PRAYING
— BY —
NUMBER

20 Creative
Prayer Lessons
& Activities

VOLUME ONE

PHYLLIS VOS WEZEMAN

 The Pastoral Center

Dedication

To Sr. Elaine DesRosiers ...

... an answer to prayer! PVW

Acknowledgment

Thanks to Jude Dennis Fournier for collaborating on the lessons and activities in the book, *Praying by Number*.

Jude is Director of Religious Formation at John the XXIII Catholic Community in Albuquerque, New Mexico. His experiences as an educator range from teaching kindergarten in Iowa and high school in Chicago to leading retreats and workshops in countless locations. Jude also serves as a Hospice Chaplain and is involved in mission in places such as El Salvador, Haiti, Kenya, and Malawi. He holds an M.A. in Spirituality.

Jude and Phyllis thrive on finding unique bakeries, coffeeshops, and dessert cafes – purely as settings for planning projects!

ISBN 978-1-949628-04-3
Printed in the United States of America.
10 9 8 7 6 5 4 3 2 1   22 21 20 19 18

The Scripture passages contained herein are from the *New Revised Standard Version of the Bible*, copyright © 1989, by the Division of Christian Education of the National Council of Churches in the U.S.A. All rights reserved.

Fleur-de-list image by Jahernan, Creative Commons Attribution-Share Alike. https://commons.wikimedia.org/wiki/File:Fleurdelis.svg.

Contents

Overview

Prayer is _____. Fill in the blank. This timeless, yet timely, question has been pondered by teachers and students throughout the ages. And, this seemingly simple statement has been completed with answers ranging from a single word to multiple volumes. Webster defines prayer as "the act of praying; an entreaty, supplication; a humble request, as to God; any set formula for this." Commentators and theologians call prayer communicating with God, opening one's life to God, engaging oneself in the purposes of God, and total immersion in the holy presence of God.

Prayer is a vital part of the Christian life. Therefore, it is a subject worth studying. We learn about prayer in many ways. By turning to Scripture, we discover how people in the Old Testament and the New Testament talked with and listened to God. We glean insight into prayer by reading stories of the saints, and we gain instruction about prayer from people of faith today. Perhaps our best guide to learning what prayer is, however, is to actually pray. And, that's what this book provides—twenty prayer opportunities for classes at church and school and for families at home. All lessons are designed to help participants explore and experience various aspects of and approaches to prayer.

This book furnishes twenty lessons based on the topic of prayer. Instruction takes place through participation as students explore and experience inviting, informing, and inspiring activities that are used to impart information and ideas. As a unique feature and a fresh approach, each lesson involves a number, from one to twenty, that becomes the focus for the experience.

Methods used to teach the subject matter incorporate architecture, art, banners/textiles, cartoons, creative writing, dance, drama, games, music, photography, puppetry, and storytelling.

Provided in an easy-to-use format, each lesson is organized into three parts:

- **Goal** states the purpose of the activity,

- **Gather** lists the materials required and suggests steps for advance preparation,

- **Guide** contains complete directions for accomplishing the task.

Prayer is for people of all ages—children, youth, and adults. While these designs are intended for young people in classroom settings, they may be easily adapted for use in small and large group worship, education, outreach, and nurture opportunities. They are ideal for parochial school programs, Sunday school classes, worship centers, children's church, vacation bible school, mid-week ministries, kids' clubs, intergenerational events, before and after school care programs, youth groups, retreats, confirmation classes, family devotions, home schooling, and more.

As you use this resource, may you be as eager and as open as Jesus' disciples were when they pleaded, "Teach us to pray." As teachers and students prepare and participate in activities, may your prayer life be enriched by discovering—or re-discovering—ways to talk with and to listen to God. As you carry the information and insight from the classroom to the world, may the power of prayer be reflected in your daily life.

① God

Goal

To involve participants in a letter writing project to be used in a "first day" prayer service, as a way to emphasize the theme "One God."

Gather

> Bible
> Candle
> Envelopes, one per person
> Equipment to play music
> Matches
> Paper, preferably stationary
> Pencils
> Pens
> Recording of tranquil music
> Stickers

Guide

On the first day of a new year, month, liturgical season (such as Lent or Advent), or significant event, like the start of school, lead the group in a creative writing activity and prayer ritual involving the theme "One God."

Begin by reading Exodus 20:3: "You shall have no other gods before me." Ask the students to name the portion of Scripture in which this text is found. The passage is commonly called "The Ten Commandments." Challenge a volunteer to identify the number of the commandment that was just recited. After someone answers "number one," explain that this law is so significant that God put it first on the list. Invite a student to summarize the meaning of the commandment in a simple phrase or sentence such as "One God"!

In Biblical times, many people prayed to idols, or "gods," of wood or stone. They thought these objects had great power and could hear their prayers. We know that a god of wood or stone has no power, can never answer prayer, and could certainly never love anyone. But God, with a capital G, can do all these things, for the Lord is the one true God, the only God. Only God can hear us and help us when we pray. Only God loves and sustains us.

Unfortunately, people sometimes have a hard time remembering and believing this simple truth. People create idols, or their own gods, every day. Modern day idols include things like clothes, hobbies, bikes, cars, super stars, and more. An idol is something that's worshiped or revered—often more than the true and only God. Take time to think about idols or gods that may be part of life. Are things like being on the soccer team, attending music concerts, or buying the best bike on the top of the list? Are they more important than God?

First days mark new beginnings. They offer a time to focus on our relationship with God, and with God's only begotten Son, Jesus. Invite the students to write a letter, in their own words, highlighting the theme "One God." These letters, to be addressed to God, are to contain promises to be kept during a designated period, such as a season, month, or year.

Ideas should center on ways the participants will put God first in their lives. Give the students an opportunity to formulate thoughts and feelings. Share examples of promises such as "I promise to spend more time reading the Bible than playing video games," or "I promise to give some of my allowance to help someone else."

Encourage the young people to be honest and to write about tangible topics such as school, family, and friends, as well as intangible ideas like joy and pain. Distribute paper and pencils and guide the group as they compose their letters.

Once the letters are written, invite the learners to sit in a circle. Light the candle and play tranquil background music. Ask the class to share the letters as a group prayer. State that each person, in turn, will have the opportunity to read her or his letter. Since the contents may be very personal, assure the group that they may read their letters out loud or silently. After everyone has had an occasion to share, conclude the ritual with a prayer asking for God's help in keeping the promises.

At the end of the prayer service distribute envelopes, stickers, and pens. Ask the students to address the envelopes to themselves, put the note inside, and seal the letter with a sticker. Collect the projects. Near the end of the designated time period, mail the letters to the participants as a reminder to live a life that honors the one true God.

❷ Prayer Partners

Goal

By painting a mandala, participants will explore two parts of prayer and will covenant (agree or commit) with another person, and with God, to become prayer partners.

Gather

- Bible
- Bible dictionary or concordance
- Containers for water
- Equipment to play music
- Paint brushes
- Paint, watercolors
- Paper for watercolor painting
- Recording of nature music

Guide

Hold up a Bible and ask the students to name its two main parts: the Old Testament and the New Testament. State that in each section of Scripture, God provides instruction on prayer. Offer two examples, one from each portion of the Bible. Use an Old Testament reference from one of the Psalms (e.g. Psalm 34:1-15) and a New Testament quotation like Matthew 21:22, or look up the word "prayer" in a concordance or Bible dictionary to find additional verses.

Next, ask the group how the number two is connected to the theme of prayer. Prayer is a two-way conversation between a person and God. Prayer involves two parts—talking and listening. Prayer can also include two people, called *prayer partners*, who commit to pray together for a specific period of time.

To make this theme meaningful for the students, explain that each person will pick a prayer partner and will make a promise to pray for and with that person for a designated period of time. Prayer partners make a covenant, or agreement, to give each other support and care. Relate examples from Scripture and from real life of this type of bond. Share the Old Testament story of Moses and Aaron's partnership (Exodus 4:14-16), and relate the New Testament account of the relationship between Mary and Elizabeth (Luke 1:39-56). Explain to the young people that partnership can mean different things. There can be a partnership with God or there can be a partnership with another person to God.

➤

If time allows, discuss listening and talking as an important part of any relationship. Ask the group questions like:

When was a time you really listened to what another person had to say?

What good came out of listening to another?

When was a time when someone really listened to you?

How did the two people benefit from the exchange?

Allow students the opportunity to share their experiences with the group.

Organize the group into pairs. Tell each pair that they will become prayer partners. Explain again that in this type of relationship each person will promise to pray for and with the other individual for a specific period of time, such as a month or a year.

As a way to seal this covenant, invite the partners to paint a mandala together. A mandala is an expression of what an individual feels on the inside while the painting is being created. Explain that both people paint at the same time; however, they do not talk to each other. The painting can be abstract or real, with both individuals contributing to the finished product.

Distribute one set of water color paints, two brushes, and one piece of water color paper to each set of prayer partners. Once the materials are dispensed, tell the participants to sit quietly with their partners. Play calm, relaxing music and invite the pairs to begin painting whatever comes to their minds. Allow time for work to take place. When all groups have finished, display the artwork for everyone to enjoy.

Conclude the session by suggesting additional opportunities to nurture the prayer partner relationship, together or apart. Partners may agree to pray for each other every morning or evening. They may also arrange to meet at a specific time each week to share joys and concerns.

❸ Trinity

Goal

To propose concrete examples of the concept of the Trinity and to construct a triptych to be used as the focal point of a personal worship center.

Gather

- Construction paper or poster board, 12" x 18"
- Examples of "three-in-one" such as apple, cube, shamrock, triangle, water
- Glue
- Greeting cards or magazines, recycled (optional)
- Paper, foil wrapping (optional)
- Picture of leader or participant
- Resource sheets:
  - "Triptych Instructions"
  - "Three-in-One Symbols"
  - "Glory Be"
- Scissors
- Trims such as braid, cording, and rick-rack (optional)

Advance Preparation

- Prepare patterns for arched panels.

Guide

Apple. Cube. Shamrock. Triangle. Water. Show the participants examples of these items and ask the group to name what they have in common. Explain that each object is three-in-one. It has three parts, and yet it is one thing. Use a cube to illustrate that our world is three dimensional—containing height, width, and depth.

Explain that while we cannot possibly ever know all there is to know about God, Christians believe that God has three ways to help us understand the Love and Light and Energy God brings to earth. We call this the Trinity, or the three-in-one concept of God: God as Father or Creator of life, God as Jesus or Redeemer of life, and God as Spirit or Sustainer of life. Explain further that this does not mean we worship three Gods, but that the Trinity is a mystery we accept by faith and understand by experience.

Invite everyone to sing or to look at the words of the "Glory Be." This song represents one of the oldest Christian expressions of the understanding of God. Explore the words as an affirmation that God is with us in all ways: as the One who creates and gives us life, as the One who saves us from our faults and sins, and as the One who is ever present with us and gives us power to live in service of God's world. God has always been and will always be whole and complete, and when we look to God in worship, that wholeness heals our brokenness and makes us one with God and each other.

If possible, hold up a picture of one of the leaders or participants. Explain that a person can be thought of as a father/mother, as a son/daughter, or as a brother/sister, yet he or she is still the same person. It just depends on the relationship being expressed. In the same way, we have different relationships with God. Encourage listeners not to worry if seeing God as three persons, yet as one God, seems confusing. Explain that they are going to participate in an activity to make the message seem more clear.

➤

Tell the participants that they are going to make a triptych, or three-fold display, that is an ancient Christian art form. The triptych was used to display three pictures or images about God or Jesus or the disciples, and to remind people of the Trinity. Each picture or image would be displayed in a separate arched panel, yet the three panels were connected.

First share the ideas to explain the Trinity, then invite participants to use those images or images of their own design to create a triptych celebrating the three-in-one concept of God.

There are many possible ways to make the idea of the Trinity seem easier to grasp. Relate as many as possible, then allow learners to use those or to develop their own to design their triptychs. Demonstrate or explain each of the following:

› **Apple.** An apple represents the Trinity in that it has three parts: the outer layer or skin, the sweet fruit, and the inner core containing the seeds.

› **Fleur-de-lis.** From French royalty comes this symbol also used as a sign of the Trinity, three flower petals, yet one flower. An iris could be used as the same symbol.

› **Pottery.** A clay pot is an earthen vessel like human beings—a trinity created by the potter's skilled hands, the wet clay, and the power of the turning wheel.

› **Shamrock.** Legend says that Saint Patrick explained the Trinity by using the three-leafed shamrock of Ireland, pointing out that it is one plant with one stem, yet it has three separate leaves.

› **Triangle.** While it is one distinct shape, a triangle is made of three sides.

› **Water** is two parts hydrogen and one-part oxygen, yet that same chemical substance can be experienced in its liquid form, or as a solid called ice, or as a vapor known as steam.

Allow the participants to choose a symbol or symbols to place on their triptych. They may separate one symbol into its parts and draw them on the different panels, or put a separate symbol on each. Another possibility would be to cut pictures from magazines or use old greeting cards to find symbols to glue on each panel. They may want to write a phrase on each panel suggesting the Trinity, such as the words to the "Glory Be," or a prayer such as "In the name of the Father who created us, the Son who redeemed us, and the Holy Spirit who lives in us." Or they may use a different prepositional phrase for each panel: "From the Father, through the Son, by the Holy Spirit."

Demonstrate the process for constructing the triptych. Fold 12" by 18" poster board or construction paper into thirds across the width. Trace a pattern to create simple arches at the top of each panel. All three sections can be the same size or the center panel can be left taller. Adding gold foil paper for a background or trimming with cord, braid, or rick-rack will add an elegant touch to the triptych. Add the chosen design to each of the three panels. Once the design is complete, tell the learners to display the triptych as the focal point of a personal worship center for use throughout the entire year.

Note: Throughout this activity, be aware that many churches are making the effort to avoid using only male images to represent God. Use wording or language that reflects the tradition and teaching of the participants. However, the opportunity should be found to explain that God is not male or female, but the creator of both. We use words like "father" because we understand God as our loving parent, the sender of all good gifts. Many cultures represent earth as our mother (as St. Francis did), although the Holy Spirit seems to represent many of the mothering or nurturing qualities of God.

Tryptych Instructions

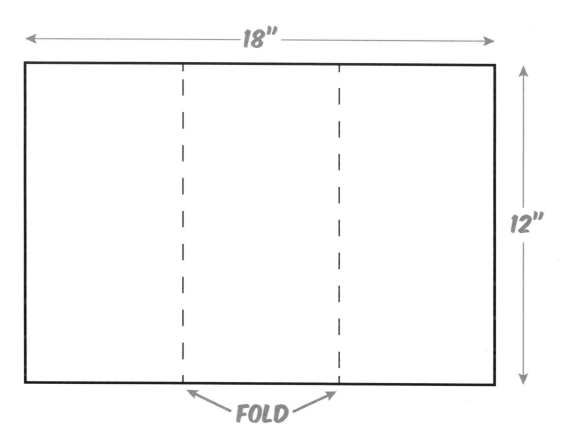

18"

12"

FOLD

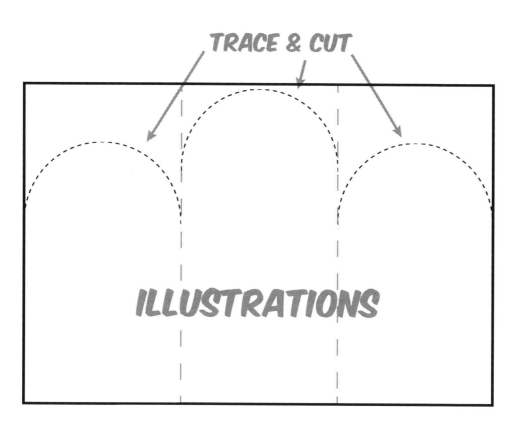

TRACE & CUT

ILLUSTRATIONS

"Three-in-One" Symbols

Glory Be

Glory be to the Father,
and to the Son,
and to the Holy Ghost;
As it was in the beginning,
is now,
and ever shall be,
world without end.
Amen!

4 Parts of Prayer

Goal

To explore four basic parts of prayer—adoration, confession, thanksgiving, and supplication—and to construct "prayer steps" as a guide for using this formula.

Gather

> Book(s) of devotions or prayers
> Chalkboard and chalk, newsprint and markers, or laptop and screen
> Dictionary
> Hymnal
> Markers
> Paper, construction
> Paper, scrap
> Pencils

Guide

Although there are many ways to create a prayer, learning a helpful formula or the basic parts or steps of prayer can be a useful guideline for students.

Begin by writing "Four _____" on a chalkboard or a sheet of newsprint. As the students arrive, have them guess, or print, possible words that could fill the blank. Of course, the answers could be four seasons, four directions, or the four evangelists. Explain that the actual answer that fits with this activity is "parts" or "steps". During this lesson the pupils will discover that there are four important parts, or steps, to every prayer.

Prayer is the way we talk to God. Sometimes a prayer can be one word, lots of words, or just a feeling in the heart. To help in conversing with God, it is useful to learn that there are four important parts of prayer:

> **Adoration** - praising God for God's greatness
> **Confession** - telling God about something that was not following God's laws
> **Thanksgiving** - thanking God for love and for gifts
> **Supplication** - asking for God's help or guidance

Organize the students into four groups and assign each cluster one part of prayer: adoration, confession, thanksgiving, and supplication. Supply the teams with resource materials, such as books of prayer, hymnals, Bibles, and dictionaries. Also provide scrap paper and pencils or pens. Direct the students to look up their assigned prayer words in the dictionary and to write definitions on the scrap paper. Instruct the learners to skim through the books to find examples of prayers that fit their respective category. Suggest checking hymnals to find songs with the "prayer" words as themes and reading the words to the hymns.

▷

Also recommend that the groups look up specific Psalms:

- Adoration: Psalm 95:1-7
- Confession: Psalm 32:1-7
- Thanksgiving: Psalm 100
- Supplication: Psalm 70:1-3,5

After a designated time, ask each group to share their discoveries about the meaning of their word and specific examples of this type of prayer.

Tell the students that they will be constructing a tool to help them use the four parts of this prayer formula: A-C-T-S. Demonstrate the procedure for creating the prayer steps. Choose a favorite color of construction paper. Fold it the short way into half, then fourths, then eighths. Open the paper and refold it on the same creases to form steps or a fan. On the bottom step, print the word "Adoration," and on the section above it write comments to demonstrate praise for God. On the next step, print "Confession," then above it enter something you need to tell God. Print "Thanksgiving" on the third step and on the section above, list reasons to be thankful. The last step is "Supplication" and the strip above can include anything for which you need God's help.

Provide the supplies and guide the students as they create their prayer steps.

Suggest that the students fold up their papers and use the craft as a bookmark. They could also stand the steps on a desk or dresser. Remind them that anytime they wish to talk to God, they can use the prayer step idea.

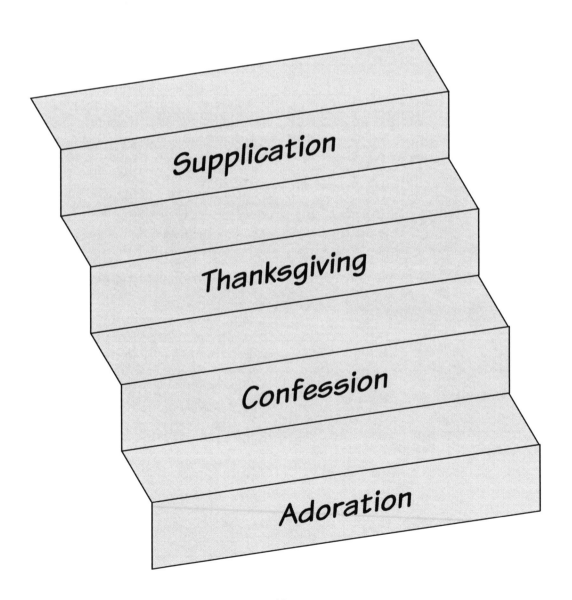

❺ Senses

Goal

To offer an opportunity to explore sight, sound, smell, taste, and touch through a prayer ritual that incorporates the five senses and to provide time for journaling on the experience.

Gather

- Bowl, large
- Bread, unleavened
- Candles, variety of sizes
- Equipment to play music
- Incense sticks
- Markers
- Matches
- Paper, newsprint
- Paper, white construction
- Pencils
- Recording of Gregorian chant music
- Tape, masking
- Water

Advance Preparation

- Purchase unleavened bread or use this recipe to make it.

Ingredients

- 3 cups whole wheat flour
- ⅔ cup honey
- ¼ stick butter
- 3 tablespoons brown sugar
- 1 teaspoon salt
- Round pan, 9"

Method

Dissolve butter and honey together until they are smooth. Add sugar and salt. Blend evenly with flour, mixing thoroughly. Mixture should be thick. Butter and flour a nine-inch round pan. Pat the dough into the prepared pan. Bake at 350 degrees for about thirty minutes. After the bread is done, flip it over in the pan and let it stand in the oven for a few minutes to remove the moisture.

Guide

Sight. Sound. Smell. Taste. Touch. God has given us five special gifts through which we experience all of life. Ask the students what these five gifts are usually called. Of course, the answer is the five senses. Invite the young people to offer examples of times when they use their five senses, such as smelling the wonderful cookies Dad is baking, tasting a gooey brownie, or petting a fluffy dog.

Organize the learners into five groups. Assign one of the senses to each team. Provide newsprint, markers, and masking tape. Explain that each group is to list on the newsprint gifts of God that they experience with their senses—sights, sounds, smells, tastes, or touches, depending on the respective assignment. Remind the participants that this is a time of brainstorming. The goal is to compile a lengthy list, not to be concerned about right and wrong answers. Give a five minute or less time frame, and a "ready, set, go" signal to begin. When the time is up, display each group's list for the group to see. Allow an opportunity to share responses.

Next, help the learners log ideas on how their senses are used in church; replies may include seeing candles, hearing music, or smelling flowers. Instruct the five groups to brainstorm and record as many ideas as possible on their newsprint sheets. At the conclusion of the designated period, allow time for sharing answers.

➤

Regather as one group. Prepare a table as the focal point for a prayer ritual by placing the following items on it: a large bowl of water, a loaf of unleavened bread, a variety of candles, an incense stick, and equipment containing a recording of Gregorian chant music. Arrange the objects in a prayerful, creative way. Give the young people an opportunity to experience each item through the gift of sight, smell, sound, taste, and touch. Explain that the items are elements of worship. One at a time, add a sensory experience to the prayer. Ignite the candle and pause to reflect on the sight. Light the incense and take time to smell the fragrance. Play the tape and allow the opportunity to enjoy its timeless sound and its echoing voices. While the music plays, invite the participants to come up, one at a time, to reverence the water. When everyone is seated, break and share the bread with each person.

After a time of silent reflection, distribute paper, pencils, construction paper, and markers to each person. Instruct the learners to form a journal by folding the papers in half, with the construction paper on the outside and the plain paper on the inside. Direct the group to record what they experienced through their five senses during the prayer ritual.

Ask the group questions like:

› What did you think of when you saw the candles burning?

› How did the bread taste to you? Did it remind you of anything?

› Did you like the smell of the incense?

› Did you ever hear Gregorian chant before?

› Did you like the way it sounded? What did it sound like?

› Was the water cold or warm to the touch? How does water feel? Does water feel different at various times?

Provide time for the learners to record their thoughts and feelings in their journals.

Continue the activity by inviting the students to journal on the following sentence starters:

Prayer looks like ...

Prayer sounds like ...

Prayer smells like ...

Prayer tastes like ...

Prayer feels like ...

Invite anyone who feels comfortable to share her or his responses with the entire group.

6 Jars of Water

Goal

To recall the story of Jesus' first miracle - turning water into wine - and to use the theme of water in six prayer activities.

Gather

> Bible
> Clay, self-hardening
> Materials related to selected activities
> Paper strips, six per person
> Pens
> Toothpicks

Guide

Count the letters in the word "prayer." There are six of them! Six is also a number associated with a special event that took place in Jesus' early ministry. This incident, recorded in the Bible in John 2:1-12, is commonly referred to as the "Miracle at Cana." Read the verses in the Gospel account and discover what the number six has to do with this story.

When Jesus, Mary, and the disciples were guests at a wedding in the town of Cana in Galilee, the host of the celebration ran out of wine. Mary immediately prompted Jesus to do something about the situation. Jesus noticed that there were stone jars—six of them—generally used for the Jewish rite of purification. Jesus instructed the servants to fill the jars with water. Then he told them to draw some of the liquid out of the containers. When the servants tasted the substance, they discovered that Jesus had turned the water to wine!

Jesus used water to perform his first miracle. And, actually, water is a miracle! Water is the substance that sustains life for everything in God's creation—even people, a word with six letters, too!

After sharing the story of the Wedding at Cana with the students, engage them in a six-part prayer activity focusing on the theme of water. Use the six suggestions for different classes, days, weeks, projects, or learning centers. Throughout this experience the group will use the theme of water to:

> discover information about projects and organizations
> name conservation methods
> recall Scripture stories
> share memories
> sing songs
> suggest uses

▷

Since there were six jars involved with Jesus' first miracle, take time to allow each person to create six simple clay containers for use during this activity. Provide balls of self-hardening clay. Tell the students to divide their clay into six portions and to follow these instructions for making jars.

Using one ball of clay, place it in the palm of the hand. Gently rotate the material around until it becomes pliable and easy to shape. Form a small jar from the clay and press an opening into the center of it. Tell the students to set the first piece aside and to repeat the process with the remaining five balls. Note that the jars do not have to be identical in size or shape. When the six jars are completed, direct the sculptors to use a toothpick to scratch a number from one to six on the outside of each jar. Allow time for the jars to harden. Distribute six small strips of paper to each person. Instruct the group to number the strips, one to six, and to write one of the following phrases on each piece:

›   Discover information
›   Name conservation methods
›   Recall Scripture stories
›   Share memories
›   Sing songs
›   Suggest uses

Tell the learners to tightly roll each strip of paper and to place the piece in the jar with the corresponding number.

Guide the group in a series of activities and prayers by having the students remove the paper from each jar, beginning with one and ending with six, and participating in a related project.

One

Direct the group to locate six Scripture stories related to the theme of water. Suggestions include:

›   Genesis 1:2 - Creation
›   Genesis 5:1-9:17 - Noah and the ark
›   Exodus 14:1-21 - Moses and the parting of the Red Sea
›   Jonah 1-2 - Jonah and the whale
›   Matthew 13:17 - Jesus' baptism in the Jordan River
›   John 2:1-11 - Jesus changes water into wine

Offer a prayer of thanks for ways in which water has been used to teach us more about God, Jesus, and the Holy Spirit.

Two

Invite the learners to name six uses of water. Suggest categories rather than specifics, such as:

›   Cleaning
›   Drinking
›   Farming
›   Industry
›   Medicinal
›   Recreation

Lead sentence prayers thanking God for ways that water is part of our lives.

➤

Three

Sing six songs related to water themes. Titles to try include:

> "Arky, Arky"
> "I've Got Peace Like a River"
> "Peace Is Flowing Like a River"
> "Rain, Rain, Go Away"
> "Raindrops Keep Falling on My Head"
> "Wide, Wide as the Ocean"

Conclude by singing "Praise God from Whom All Blessings Flow," concentrating on the theme of water as a gift from God.

Four

Explain the need for water conservation. Challenge the group to name six ways to preserve this crucial resource. Possible answers are:

> Plant trees
> Repair leaks
> Run full loads of laundry
> Sweep rather than hose sidewalks
> Take short showers
> Use water saving appliances

Guide the group in praying that they may be good stewards of God's gift of water.

Five

Share memories of experiences in which water was the focus. Ask each person to relate a remembrance based on these six, or other, suggestions:

> Fun
> People
> Pets
> Places
> Thirst
> Vacation

Use a popcorn prayer, with each person interjecting one word at a time, recounting memories of water-related experiences.

Six

Share information about service projects that offer water to "thirsty" people:

> Agricultural education
> Fish farms
> Homeless centers
> Irrigation projects
> Soup kitchens
> World relief organizations

Pray for people who share God's love by participating in water related projects.

At the conclusion of the six activities, suggest that the students set their jars in a special place and that they use the information and ideas to remember the importance of God's wondrous gift of water.

7 Gifts of the Spirit

Goal

To use guided meditation to help participants discern the seven gifts of the Spirit: wisdom, understanding, counsel (right judgment), knowledge, fortitude (courage), reverence (piety), and fear of the Lord (wonder and awe).

Gather

> Bibles
> Candles, seven of various colors and sizes
> Markers
> Matches
> Resource sheet
  > "Gifts of the Spirit: Guided Meditation"
> Resources about the "Gifts of the Spirit"

Guide

One of God's great gifts to believers is the Holy Spirit. And the Holy Spirit—the third person of the Trinity—bestows upon Christians seven special characteristics, traditionally referred to as the Gifts of the Spirit.

Listed in various places in the New Testament, especially 1 Corinthians 12:8-10, and prophesied in the Old Testament in Isaiah 11:1-3, God has shared these gifts with people by sending the Spirit to help God's followers live Christ-like lives.

Using newsprint and markers, challenge the students to identify the seven historical Gifts of the Spirit. Write the names of the "gifts" they identify, even if incorrect. Ask the learners to explain why they chose the gifts they mentioned. Once all the pupils have had an opportunity to participate, write the seven gifts on a clean sheet of newsprint.

>

Look up a Scripture reference related to each gift and use the following ideas as a guide for discussion:

Wisdom

"The Lord gives wisdom." (Proverbs 2:6)

Wisdom helps us make right decisions and guides us from doing wrong. Wisdom is a gift people build up through experience. A wise person knows what to do in many situations. A wise believer sees the people and events of human history fitting together in the large plan of God's love.

Understanding

"Give me understanding so I may keep your law with all my heart." (Psalm 119:34)

Understanding helps us discover what the stories in the Bible, especially Jesus' instructions, have to teach us. Understanding is the gift of thinking and reflecting on experience. People with understanding think things through for themselves and act on their insights.

Counsel (Right Judgment)

"How wonderful is the Lord's judgment." (Isaiah 28:29)

This gift helps us to lead others in knowing what is right and wrong and how to be courageous in doing what is right. Counsel is a willingness to consider the insights and understandings of others about a situation and to work together towards a solution.

Knowledge

"The earth shall be filled with the knowledge of the Lord." (Isaiah 11:9)

The gift of knowledge helps us to know Jesus as our friend and to comprehend what is needed to serve God. Knowledge is a gift for seeking out the facts and information necessary to make wise and fair decisions.

Fortitude (Courage)

"Be strong in the Lord and in the strength of his power." (Ephesians 6:10)

This gift helps us to love God and others and to do what God wants us to do, even when we are afraid. Courage is the strength to do what isn't always easy, to stand up for the unpopular, to speak the truth, to put one's self on the line for what is right.

Reverence (Piety)

"Reverence the Lord Christ in your heart." (1 Peter 3:15)

Reverence helps us to show our love for God, God's people, and God's earth in our words and actions. Reverence is the gift of honoring God and others. The pious person reveres and worships God. The pious person has reverence for all people with the respect we want for ourselves.

Fear of the Lord (Wonder/Awe)

"Reverence the holy One and be in awe of the God of Israel." (Isaiah 29:23)

This gift helps us put God first in everything we say and do and show respect for God's holy name and all of creation. Fear of the Lord is the gift of awe and wonder at God's life-giving and life-sustaining presence in creation and in us.

➤

The Journey of Life

Also, discuss ways in which these statements reflect the journey of life. Share the following lines:

> I am seeking wisdom.
> I see a need for a deep understanding.
> I know I need good judgment to be the best I can be.
> I could use a good dose of courage, too.
> Knowledge won't come easily. I must work for it.
> I really want to be respectful and reverent.
> It can be wonderful and awesome to be alive and to have faith.

Guided Meditation

Tell the group that they will participate in a Guided Meditation as a way of reflecting on each of the seven gifts of the Spirit. Invite the participants to form a circle on the floor or on chairs and to sit in a comfortable position. Place the seven candles in the center of the circle. Light one candle after each of the gifts is mentioned.

Before beginning the meditation invite the students to pray the following words, repeating each line:

> *Come, Holy Spirit,*
> *fill the hearts of your people*
> *and enkindle in them the fire of your love.*
> *Send forth your Spirit*
> *and you shall renew the face of the earth.*
> *Amen.*

Continue the experience by reading the guided meditation found on the handout slowly and prayerfully. Light each candle at the appropriate time in the reading.

After the guided meditation, direct the students to pause in complete silence to allow time to wonder prayerfully about what they have just heard and visualized. Invite the participants to say a silent prayer of thanks for the gifts of the Spirit and for the ways in which these blessings help them live a Christ-like life. Tell them to open their eyes when they are ready.

Conclude the session by quietly repeating the prayer to the Holy Spirit used at the beginning of the Guided Meditation or by reciting the following prayer from the Rite of Confirmation #25:

> *All powerful God,*
> *   the Father of our Lord Jesus Christ,*
> *by water and the Holy Spirit*
> *   you freed your sons and daughters from sin*
> *   and gave them new life.*
>
> *Send your Holy Spirit upon them*
> *   to be their Helper and Guide.*
>
> *Give them the spirit of wisdom*
> *   and understanding,*
> *the spirit of right judgment and courage,*
> *the spirit of knowledge and reverence.*
>
> *Fill them with the spirit of wonder*
> *   and awe in your presence.*
>
> *We ask this through Christ our Lord.*
>
> *Amen.*

Gifts of the Spirit: Guided Meditation

God the Holy Spirit, the third Person of the Trinity, is with us today. To help us, the Holy Spirit gives us special gifts so that this day and every day we can make good decisions.

Wisdom

The Holy Spirit gives us wisdom.

(Light the first candle.)

Think for a moment of a time when you knew what God wanted of you and you did it. See in your mind what it was that you did.

Understanding

The Holy Spirit gives us understanding.

(Light the second candle.)

Think for a moment of a time when you showed compassion and understanding toward another person. What was the situation? Recall it in your mind.

Counsel/Right Judgment

The Holy Spirit gives us the gift of counsel or right judgment.

(Light the third candle.)

Think for a moment of a time when you made the right decision. In your mind see who was involved in this decision. Was it many people or just you and God?

Courage

The Holy Spirit gives us courage, also called fortitude.

(Light the fourth candle.)

Think for a moment of a time when you did something that took a lot of courage. Perhaps it was standing up for something you believed in. In your mind and heart what did it feel like? Were you afraid?

Knowledge

The Spirit gives us the gift of knowledge.

(Light the fifth candle.)

Think for a moment of a time when you had clear knowledge of God and your faith. In your mind see once again how God was made known.

Reverence

The Spirit gives us reverence.

(Light the sixth candle.)

Think for a moment of a time when you were filled with a deep love for God. In your mind see where God is in your life. Do you feel God's presence right now?

Wonder and Awe

The Holy Spirit gives us the gift of wonder and awe.

(Light the seventh candle.)

Think for a moment of a time when you were filled with wonder and awe at God's creation. In your mind see your favorite place in the world. With your eyes closed, be in that place for a moment or two. Give thanks to God for his wonderful gifts.

⑧ Beatitudes

Goal

By participating in different prayer postures, students will experience a deeper understanding of the eight Beatitudes.

Gather

- › Bibles
- › Equipment to play music
- › Paper, one sheet per person
- › Pencils or pens
- › Recording of tranquil music
- › Resource sheets:
  - › "The Beatitudes"
  - › "The Beatitudes: Prayer Postures"

Guide

An overture introduces and plays various themes of the symphony or the music that follows. A hint here... full promise there... a startling burst of color. So it is with the Beatitudes. They are the overture to the Sermon on the Mount.

Begin by asking the students questions about the Sermon on the Mount.

- › Why was the Sermon so important?
- › What was Jesus saying in this message?
- › What are the Beatitudes?
- › How do the Beatitudes ask us to be different?
- › Why do you think Jesus gave us the Beatitudes?

Encourage discussion before distributing copies of the first Beatitudes resource sheet to the participants or asking them to look up the verses, Matthew 5:1-10, in their Bibles.

Understanding Each Beatitude

Pass out a copy of the Beatitudes to each learner. Invite eight participants to read the statements aloud. Encourage dialogue after each Beatitude is read. Guide the group in thinking about what Jesus' words mean for people today. Use the following thoughts to direct the conversation.

"Blessed are the poor in spirit, for theirs is the kingdom of heaven."

To be poor in spirit is to remember that we cannot depend on things or possessions, but only on God and God's unfailing love.

"Blessed are those who mourn, for they will be comforted."

To mourn is to be sad and to sometimes cry when we see people who are hurting and in pain because of sin, hatred, sickness, death, poverty, war, or injustice.

➤

*"Blessed are the meek,
for they will inherit the earth."*

To be meek is to be humble and to realize that all our gifts, talents, and abilities come from God. We need to use them to do good for others and to make a better world for all people.

"Blessed are those who hunger and thirst for righteousness, for they will be filled."

To hunger and thirst for righteousness is to have a great desire to do what God requires of us—to see that justice is carried out. It is to work for good relationships between people and peace in the entire world.

*"Blessed are the merciful,
for they will receive mercy."*

To be merciful is to show love and compassion to people in need and to forgive those who hurt us.

*"Blessed are the pure in heart,
for they will see God."*

To be clean of heart is to put God first in our lives and to do what we know is right.

*"Blessed are the peacemakers,
for they will be called children of God."*

To be a peacemaker is to always try to be reconciled or at peace with others, even if they are our enemies. To forgive and to be forgiven is very important in being a peacemaker.

*"Blessed are those who are persecuted
for righteousness' sake,
for theirs is the kingdom of heaven."*

To be persecuted because we do what God asks is to have the strength and courage to do what Jesus teaches us, no matter who ridicules or punishes us for living as Jesus lived.

Beatitude Prayer Gestures

As a way to further illustrate the Beatitudes and to provide a prayer experience based on Jesus' important words, invite the students to be seated on the floor. Dim the lights and put on soft music. Encourage and lead the participants in a different prayer posture, or gesture, for each of the Beatitudes, as found on the resource sheet.

Once the exercise is completed, invite the students to sit quietly and to reflect on the experience. After an appropriate time, distribute a piece of paper and a pencil to each person. Tell the pupils to record their thoughts and feelings about what they learned from the Beatitudes and from praying Jesus' teachings through gesture and movement. If individuals feel comfortable sharing their responses, encourage conversation from the group after the activity.

The Beatitudes

Matthew 5:1-10

When Jesus saw the crowds, he went up the mountain;
and after he sat down, his disciples came to him.
Then he began to speak, and taught them, saying:

Blessed are the poor in spirit,
for theirs is the kingdom of heaven.

Blessed are those who mourn,
for they will be comforted.

Blessed are the meek,
for they will inherit the earth.

Blessed are those who hunger and thirst for righteousness,
for they will be filled.

Blessed are the merciful,
for they will receive mercy.

Blessed are the pure in heart,
for they will see God.

Blessed are the peacemakers,
for they will be called children of God.

Blessed are those who are persecuted for righteousness' sake,
for theirs is the kingdom of heaven.

The Beatitudes: Prayer Postures

*"Blessed are the poor in spirit,
for theirs is the kingdom of heaven."*

Fold arms across chest. Extend arms toward heaven.

*"Blessed are those who mourn,
for they will be comforted."*

Place hands over face. Embrace shoulders.

*"Blessed are the meek,
for they will inherit the earth."*

Kneel, arms down, palms out, towards earth.

*"Blessed are those who hunger and thirst for righteousness,
for they will be filled."*

Outstretch arms and hands. Stand.

*"Blessed are the merciful,
for they will receive mercy."*

Bow head with hands folded in prayer.

*"Blessed are the pure of heart,
for they will see God."*

Cup hands over the heart, head up with eyes open to heaven.

*"Blessed are the peacemakers,
for they will be called children of God."*

Make a circle by joining hands. Lift hands over head.

*"Blessed are those who are persecuted
for righteousness' sake,
for theirs is the kingdom of heaven."*

Kneel with hands outstretched in front of body.
Stand with head and hands toward heaven.

❾ Fruit of the Spirit

Goal

To review the nine fruit of the Spirit and to dramatize stories of biblical, historical, and modern-day people who evidence love, joy, peace, patience, kindness, goodness, faithfulness, gentleness, and self-control in their lives.

Gather

> Bibles
> Candles and holders
> Costume pieces
> Matches
> Paper
> Pencils or pens
> Props
> Resource materials on biblical, historical, and modern-day people of faith

Guide

Galatians 5:22-23 identifies nine fruit of the Spirit. Look up the passage and read the list: love, joy, peace, patience, kindness, goodness, faithfulness, gentleness, and self-control. Explain that the fruit of the Spirit are the outward expressions of faith in a person's life; they are the external evidence of the work of the Holy Spirit in the life of a believer. The fruit of the Spirit are also characteristics displayed by people of prayer.

Challenge the participants to think of people whose lives exhibit love, joy, peace, patience, kindness, goodness, faithfulness, gentleness, and self-control. Tell the students that they will use Scripture stories, biographical information, and resource materials to match a biblical, historical, or modern-day person of prayer with each fruit of the Spirit. Provide examples to start the project, such as:

Love

> Biblical: Jesus
> Historical: Saint Margaret of Scotland
> Modern-day: Mother Teresa

Joy

> Biblical: Elizabeth
> Historical: Saint Nicholas
> Modern-day: Amy Grant

Peace

> Biblical: Noah
> Historical: Saint Francis
> Modern-Day: Gandhi

Patience

> Biblical: Job
> Historical: Annie Sullivan (Helen Keller's teacher)
> Modern-Day: Corrie Ten Boom

▶

Kindness

- Biblical: Abraham
- Historical: Clara Barton
- Modern-day: Jane Addams

Goodness

- Biblical: Lydia
- Historical: Abraham Lincoln
- Modern-day: Jimmy Carter

Faithfulness

- Biblical: Ruth
- Historical: Saint Patrick
- Modern-day: Oscar Romero

Gentleness

- Biblical: Mary
- Historical: Anne Frank
- Modern-day: Eleanor Roosevelt

Self-control

- Biblical: Paul
- Historical: Dietrich Bonhoeffer
- Modern-day: Martin Luther King, Jr.

Have the participants work on this project in one of the following ways:

- Work individually, finding one example for each "fruit."
- Work in small groups, with each identifying a person for each "fruit" or for one specific "fruit."
- Have one group research biblical people, another group identify historical individuals, and the third group study modern-day men, women, youth, and children.

Provide Bibles and books, as well as paper and pencils or pens. Guide the students as they search the Scriptures and the sources and gather information on the people they select.

Once the information has been compiled, re-gather the large group. Make a list of the people who were identified for each fruit of the Spirit. Take time to discuss ways in which the characteristic is evidenced in the person's life. For example, Mother Teresa demonstrates love through her self-sacrificing work with the poor.

Ruth displays faithfulness by remaining with her mother-in-law, Naomi.

Choose one person on the list to illustrate each quality—love, joy, peace, patience, kindness, goodness, faithfulness, gentleness, and self-control—by asking the participants to vote by raising their hands, applauding, or voicing their opinions. Try to include three biblical, three historical, and three modern-day examples in the final selections.

Tell the learners that they will use nine different forms of drama to briefly illustrate the stories of the biblical, historical, and modern-day persons and that they will incorporate these sketches into a prayer service. Organize the learners into nine groups and assign one fruit of the Spirit/person of prayer and one dramatic method to each team. Dramatic methods to try include:

- Characterization of Bible passage
- First person
- Improvisation
- Interview
- Masks
- Mime
- News report
- Role play
- Tableau

Provide time and materials and help the small groups prepare their presentations for the prayer service. When the participants are ready, assemble the students in an area prepared for the worship experience.

Begin the service by lighting the first candle and saying, "The fruit of the Spirit are..." Name the first fruit: love. Invite the participants who prepared the love segment to present their dramatic sketch. After the story, allow time for silent reflection on the message. Invite the group to respond with the words: "Thank you, God for the example of [name person]. Help us to show love in our lives."

Repeat the process until the nine candles have been lit, dramas have been presented, and the responses have been spoken. Conclude by re-reading Galatians 5:22-23 to the group.

⑩ Commandments

This is NOT Catholic !

Goal

Through the use of an action story, participants will review the Ten Commandments and respond to God's laws as guidelines for prayer.

Gather

> Chalk or markers (optional)
> Chalkboard or newsprint (optional)
> Resource sheet:
>> "Ten Commandments Action Story"

Guide

Prayer is one method of expressing love for God and for others. Living a life based on the Ten Commandments is another. In Exodus 20:1-17 and Deuteronomy 5:1-22, God gives us instructions for showing love for our Creator and for all human beings. Jesus summarized the Old Testament laws with the New Testament words "Love God with all your heart, and your neighbor as yourself" (Matthew 22:37-40). Communicating love for God and for others through adoration, confession, thanksgiving, and supplication, should be the essence of every prayer. Use this lesson to help the learners understand the relationship between prayer and the Ten Commandments.

Study the Ten Commandments and help the students make a commitment to live according to God's guidelines. While it can be helpful to memorize significant portions of Scripture, it is more important to understand the meaning behind the words. Review the Ten Commandments in a unique way by using an action story. An action story includes movements and gestures to illustrate each line. It involves the learner in the process and assures that the Bible story is memorable and meaningful.

After explaining the theme of the lesson, have the group sit or stand facing the leader who tells the story and demonstrates all motions for the participants. Words to be repeated can be written on newsprint or on a chalkboard or can simply be emphasized with the voice so that hearers understand the key word to repeat. Additional movements and gestures may be improvised by the group or the leader. Review the Ten Commandments using the words found on the resource sheet.

At the conclusion of the action story, ask the group to name ways that the Ten Commandments relate to the topic of prayer. Of course, everyone needs to pray for God's help and guidance in keeping the laws. And since we cannot keep the Commandments perfectly, we must pray for forgiveness when we break them. Most importantly, be sure the students understand that the theme of love for God and for others, as outlined in the Ten Commandments, must be the basis for all prayer.

10 Commandments Action Story

Not Catholic! Do not use unless modify commandments

 Commandment number one
is simple to recall:
There is only one God
Jehovah, Lord of all.
[Raise one finger.]

 Commandment number two
has good advice for you.
Do not serve any idols.
There's just one God that's true.
[Raise two fingers.]

 God's name is very special
hold it in high regard.
That's commandment number three.
That isn't very hard.
[Raise three fingers.]

 The Sabbath is a special day.
Do not work, but rest.
The fourth commandment tells us
that the Sabbath is the best.
[Raise four fingers.]

 Your father and your mother
are gifts from God to you.
Commandment number five says
honor them in all you do.
[Raise five fingers.]

  Do not murder is number six,
the commandment after five.
The special creatures God has made
must all be kept alive.
[Raise six fingers.]

  Be faithful to the one you love
is seven's guide for life.
This is a good commandment
for a husband and a wife.
[Raise seven fingers.]

  Commandment eight says do not take
what does not belong to you.
By keeping this commandment
you praise God in all you do.
[Raise eight fingers.]

 Don't bear false witness, number nine
means in everything you do
tell the truth about others.
It is God's law for you.
[Raise nine fingers.]

 There may be things that others have
that you'd like to have too.
Number ten says do not covet.
This is God's guide for you.
[Raise ten fingers.]

⑪ The Lord's Prayer

Goal

Through the use of creative writing and mantra, participants will take a closer look at the Lord's Prayer—the model for all Christian prayer.

Gather

> Bibles, one per person (optional)
> Markers
> Newsprint
> Tape, masking

Guide

Often, the Lord's Prayer is repeated rotely and routinely. When this happens, it becomes nothing more than empty words, and, unfortunately, Jesus' important teachings are missed. The Lord's Prayer—Jesus' lesson to us on prayer—is an affirmation of God's abundant and unending love for God's children. This learning activity will help participants meditate on each petition and will encourage a better understanding of the words of this wonderful guide for our devotional life.

Ask the students to identify the only prayer in the Bible that Jesus taught us to pray. Wait for answers. Once the Lord's Prayer has been mentioned, ask if anyone knows where it is located in the New Testament. To help the pupils, distribute Bibles. If the learners are having difficulty finding the verses, suggest that they look in Luke's Gospel. Ask them to continue the search. If the participants still need help, direct them to chapter 11. The Lord's Prayer is at the beginning of this chapter. Ask participants to read Luke 11:2-4 silently. Once all have read the passage, invite one student to read the verses out loud to the entire group.

Take 11 sheets of newsprint and print one line of the Lord's Prayer on each sheet. The lines should be written as follows:

Our Father who art in heaven...
Hallowed be thy name...
Thy kingdom come...
Thy will be done...
On earth...
As it is in heaven...
Give us this day our daily bread...
And forgive us our trespasses...
As we forgive those who trespass against us...
And lead us not into temptation...
But deliver us from evil.

Tape the newsprint sheets, in order, to the walls of the room.

➤

Invite the students to continue exploring the meaning of the Lord's Prayer by adding their own words after each of the eleven lines. This may be done as an individual or group project, depending on the size of the class.

For example, the entire group may discuss ideas and one person may write responses on the sheets, or small groups of two or three students may be assigned to record their thoughts on one specific piece of newsprint. As an individual project, ask each pupil to stand at a different piece of paper. At a designated signal, instruct the participants to write their thoughts on the assigned theme. Time the activity, and after one minute, direct the students to move one sheet to the right and to repeat the process. Continue the activity until each person has had the opportunity to record responses for each of the eleven phrases.

Before beginning the activity review examples such as:

Our Father who are in heaven...

> *You are only God.*
> *Jesus asked us to call you "Father," and so we do.*
> *You look after our world.*
> *You are the one who, out of love, gave us our life.*
> *You wait for the day to see all your people in heaven.*

Hallowed be thy name...

> *All of creation is holy and good because of your awesome power and goodness.*
> *Blessed and holy is your name, you who are the source of all love.*
> *Help us remember we can do nothing without you.*
> *Abba Father, I love your name.*

Thy kingdom come...

> *We try hard at building your kingdom.*
> *Your kingdom ... a place where all people will live in harmony with one another and with your wonderful earth.*
> *Your kingdom ... a place where peace and understanding will be the rule.*

Thy will be done...

> *Your will, not mine, Lord.*
> *If you lead I will go, I will follow in your way.*
> *Father, you gave us a free will. Help us to do our part in changing this imperfect world.*
> *Make my heart as yours, open and willing, one and the same.*
> *Your will be done in my life.*

On earth...

> *On earth, yes, Lord, may all that you stood for be lived out here on earth.*
> *We want our life on earth to please you.*
> *We know, dear God, and we have experienced pieces of your kingdom here on earth.*

As it is in heaven...

> *Heaven God? Sometimes I wonder.*
> *There's so much pain, so much hate, so much violence.*
> *We know you're there, somewhere. In heaven?*

Give us this day our daily bread...

> *Each day is a gift.*
> *Give us the hope we need to understand.*
> *Continue to feed us with the goodness of your life, the life of Jesus who came to give food to all people.*
> *Bread for weary travelers... soul food.*
> *Give to us today and all our days the compassion to feed those who have no hope.*

And forgive us our trespasses...

> *God we have done wrong, we have hurt others, we have not loved.*
> *Help those we have hurt to forgive us.*
> *Help us to forgive ourselves.*
> *We fail most of the time at not seeing Jesus in other people.*
> *We have lied and shown hate.*
> *Fill us with virtue, help us to love in all ways.*
> *Look into our hearts and find the goodness.*
> *We ask to be forgiven.*

➤

As we forgive those who trespass against us...

> *To do as Jesus did is difficult at times.*

> *To forgive isn't easy.*

> *What! When someone hurts me and puts me down, I need to forgive?!*

> *Help us in this forgiveness thing.*

> *Help us to see and accept the weakness in others.*

> *Help us to realize that imperfection is a part of being human.*

> *In a world where ME and I are most important, and US and WE are a thing of the past, help us to put things into the proper perspective.*

And lead us not into temptation...

> *We need your help Lord. Temptation is all around us.*

> *We pray that we will be spared the allurements of evil.*

> *We recall how Jesus was tempted but never gave in.*

> *Lead us into that same strength.*

> *Lead us onto the right path - The path of courage and compassion.*

But deliver us from evil. Amen.

> *Evil seems to be all around us.*

> *This is not the world you want.*

> *Drugs, killing, hate, using other people for our own pleasure, lying, stealing all come so easy.*

> *Lord, the evil one is all around, waiting to take us in.*

> *Deliver us from all that is evil and bring all of life to holy completion.*

Once the creative writing activity is completed, take time to review the ideas recorded on each sheet of newsprint.

As a conclusion to this unique learning experience, invite the participants to sit in a circle and lead the group in a mantra, or chant, of the Lord's Prayer. Slowly and thoughtfully say each line of the prayer, asking the students to meditatively and reflectively repeat each line as it is spoken. End the activity with a quiet dismissal.

⑫ The Apostles' Creed

Goal

To explore the twelve articles of the Apostles' Creed through participation in an architecture/art project and to incorporate symbol rubbings into a year-long prayer calendar.

Gather

> Calendar containing separate months of the year
> Copy machine
> Crayons, large unwrapped dark colors
> Glue
> Markers
> Newsprint
> Objects related to articles of The Apostles' Creed such as:

>> Alpha & Omega (1)
>> Butterfly (5)
>> Chalice (10)
>> Circle (12)
>> Cloud (6)
>> Cross (10)
>> Crown (6)
>> Crown of Thorns (4)
>> Dove (8)
>> Fire (7)
>> Fish (9)
>> Lamb (4)
>> Lily (3)
>> Manger (3)
>> Olive Tree (12)
>> Phoenix (11)
>> Ship (9)
>> Symbol: IHS (2)
>> Symbol: XP (2)
>> Tomb, open (5)
>> Triangle (8)
>> Trumpet (7)
>> Wheat (11)
>> World (1)

> Paper, 5" x 8" pieces
> Paper, 11" x 17" sheets - seven per participant
> Resource sheet:
>> "The Apostles' Creed"
> Scissors
> Stapler
> Staples
> Tape, masking

Advance Preparation

> Refer to the resource sheet and print each article on a separate sheet of newsprint.
> Collect objects relevant to the articles of the Apostle's Creed. Use the list in the Gather section of the lesson as a guide.
> Duplicate a set of months of the year for each calendar/participant.
> Select details in a church or school that will make interesting rubbings: cornerstones, engravings, and plaques.
> Request permission to use objects in the church or school for this activity.

Guide

Since we know the Bible is so important to our faith, we try to memorize parts of Scripture. Although we can't memorize every word of the Bible, early Christians wrote statements based on the truths in God's Word that people could memorize. Those declarations are called "creeds," or short statements of belief. One often-used creed is the "Apostles' Creed," twelve articles that summarize the most important scriptural teachings of the Apostles, Jesus' first followers.

Challenge the students to "recite" the Apostles' Creed in a unique way. Give each person, or team, one of the twelve pieces of newsprint— each containing an article of the Creed—that were prepared in advance. Direct the participants to line up in the order the phrases appear in the creed. The student or group with the words "I believe in God the Father almighty..." should be at the beginning of the line and the pupil or team with the phrase "And the life everlasting..." should be at the end of the queue. Give a "ready, set, go" signal and guide the players as they complete the sequencing activity.

➤

The proper order is:

1. *I believe in God, the Father almighty, Creator of Heaven and earth,*
2. *and in Jesus Christ, His only Son, Our Lord,*
3. *who was conceived by the Holy Spirit, born of the Virgin Mary,*
4. *suffered under Pontius Pilate, was crucified, died, and was buried;*
5. *he descended into hell; the third day he rose again from the dead;*
6. *he ascended into heaven, and is seated at the right hand of God, the Father almighty;*
7. *from thence he shall come to judge the living and the dead.*
8. *I believe in the Holy Spirit,*
9. *the holy Catholic Church, the communion of saints,*
10. *the forgiveness of sins,*
11. *the resurrection of the body*
12. *and life everlasting.*

Once the pupils and the phrases are arranged, ask each group to read the words they are holding.

Suggest that one way to remember the words of each article of the Apostles' Creed is to associate a symbol with it. Instruct each group to re-read the words they are holding and direct the students to try to think of a symbol that could represent the phrase. Encourage the learners to help each other with suggestions. Possible symbols include:

I believe in God, the Father almighty, Creator of heaven and earth,
> Alpha and Omega
> world

and in Jesus Christ, his only Son, our Lord,
> IHS, the first letters of Jesus' name in Greek capitals
> XP, the first two letters of the Greek word for Christ

who was conceived by the Holy Spirit, born of the Virgin Mary,
> lily
> manger

suffered under Pontius Pilate, was crucified, died, and was buried;
> crown of thorns
> lamb

he descended into hell; on the third day he rose again from the dead;
> butterfly
> open tomb

he ascended into heaven, and seated at the right hand of God the Father almighty;
> cloud
> crown

from there he will come to judge the living and the dead.
> fire
> trumpet

I believe in the Holy Spirit,
> dove
> triangle

The holy catholic Church, the communion of saints,
> fish
> ship

The forgiveness of sins,
> chalice
> cross

the resurrection of the body,
> phoenix
> wheat

and life everlasting. Amen.
> circle
> olive tree

> ▷

One way to remember the symbols for the Apostles' Creed is to make a rubbing. This ancient art form captures architectural details on paper. Explain that each person will rub a symbol for each phrase of the Creed. Later, the artwork will be combined into a twelve-month calendar activity to help illustrate the twelve articles.

Demonstrate the process for making a rubbing. Place thin paper over the symbol and use masking tape to hold the paper in place. Rub firmly over the paper using a crayon held on its side. Use broad strokes until the complete image appears.

Gather the group in the location where the rubbings will be done. If possible, use the inside and the outside of the church or school so the architectural details of the building can be incorporated into the rubbings. This project may also be executed around tables or on the floor by providing objects to trace. Supply paper and crayons and guide the students as they work.

Once the pupils have completed twelve rubbings, re-gather the group and provide instructions for combining the art projects into a twelve-month calendar—one page for each article of the Creed. Furnish seven pieces of paper for each calendar. Large size paper such as 11" x 17" allows the students room for the illustrations. Fold the seven pages in half and staple the sheets in the middle, on the crease line. Use the twelve top sections of the calendar to mount the symbols. Note that the emblems may have to be trimmed to fit in the space. Tell the participants to write the words of the respective article of the Creed on the sheet.

To make the pages for each month, dates may be copied from another calendar, or calendar pages may be duplicated and glued to the bottom of each respective sheet. Design a cover, including the words "The Apostles' Creed."

Tell the students to display their completed calendars in a place that will serve as a reminder that the Apostles' Creed is our statement of what we believe about God's Word and God's promises. The Apostles' Creed, and the symbols associated with each article, help us to say easily and quickly what we believe as Christians.

The Apostles' Creed

I believe in God,
the Father almighty,
Creator of heaven and earth,
and in Jesus Christ, his only Son, our Lord,
who was conceived by the Holy Spirit,
born of the Virgin Mary,
suffered under Pontius Pilate,
was crucified, died and was buried;
he descended into hell;
on the third day he rose again from the dead;
he ascended into heaven,
and is seated at the right hand of God the Father almighty;
from there he will come to judge the living and the dead.

I believe in the Holy Spirit,
the holy catholic Church,
the communion of saints,
the forgiveness of sins,
the resurrection of the body,
and life everlasting.

Amen.

⓭ Disciples

Goal

To review information about Jesus' thirteen disciples, the original twelve plus Matthias, and to create newspapers containing examples of their experiences of prayer.

Gather

> Bibles
> Glue
> Markers
> Paper, construction or newsprint – 11" x 17" or 12" x 18"
> Pencils and pens
> Scissors

Guide

"Extra! Extra! Read all about it! Special edition on Jesus' disciples!" Invite the participants to become "reporters" and to create newspapers containing information about Jesus and his special followers, especially their times of prayer. Begin by asking how many disciples Jesus had. Most likely, participants will answer "twelve." Twelve is a correct answer since at any one time there were twelve disciples. Actually, thirteen men were chosen to be the special helpers of Jesus. Ask the pupils to try to name them: Simon Peter, Andrew, James, John, Philip, Bartholomew, Matthew, Thomas, James the Less, Jude/Thaddaeus, Simon the Zealot, Judas Iscariot, and Matthias (the replacement for Judas Iscariot).

Remind the students that a disciple is a pupil or follower of a teacher or school. In this activity, the word "disciple" refers to an early follower of Jesus, especially the original twelve and the one replacement, often called the Apostles. One of Jesus' most notable teachings to this group was on the topic of prayer. Prayer was an important part of Jesus' life. In fact, because the selection of the first disciples was such a significant consideration, Jesus spent the entire night praying to God before he came to his decision (Luke 6:12-13). Read the passage to the class.

Organize the "reporters" into five groups to learn more about the theme of prayer. Provide each team with a Bible, paper, and pencils or pens, and assign one of the Gospels and Acts passages to each group. Tell the students that these books record what Jesus teaches us about prayer—why we should pray, how to pray, and when to pray. Direct the participants to scan their assigned book to find examples of prayer involving Jesus and the disciples.

➤

Illustrations include:

- *Matthew 6:9-15 - Jesus teaches the disciples to pray*
- *Mark 14:22-26 -- Jesus prays at the Last Supper*
- *Luke 22:39-46 - Jesus prays in Gethsemane*
- *John 17:20-26 - Jesus prays for all His followers*
- *Acts 1:12-26 - The disciples pray before choosing a replacement*

Using a newspaper format, instruct each group to create and complete projects for their own edition of *The Galilee Gazette*. Provide each team with a large sheet of paper such as newsprint, construction paper, or copy paper. Direct attention to additional supplies such as paper, markers, scissors, and glue.

Challenge the teams to compose articles and to create illustrations describing the prayer experiences contained in their assigned book. Suggest an editorial on the importance of prayer, a classified ad containing the job description of a disciple as a person of prayer, a map of the area in which Jesus and the disciples ministered, or a pictorial essay on one of Jesus' teachings on prayer. After pictures are drawn, stories are written, or activities are completed, the "layout" should be arranged in an attractive format and attached to the newspaper sheet.

Once the newspapers are compiled, ask each team to pass their reports to the group to their right. Allow time for the students to review each other's work. Continue passing projects until each group has read all five newspapers. Conclude by asking individuals to identify the differences and the similarities contained in each of the accounts.

⑭ Works of Mercy

Goal

Participants will review the fourteen Works of Mercy - seven Corporal and seven Spiritual guides for showing love for God, self, and others - and construct a Prayer Prompter to use as a reminder to put the words into action.

Gather

> Construction paper
> Copy machine
> Markers
> Newsprint or poster board
> Paper, 8 ½" x 11"
> Pens
> Resource sheet
> > "Prayer Prompter"
> Rulers
> Scissors

Advance Preparation

> Cut construction paper into 4 ½" x 12" pieces, 1 per person.
> Cut 4" x 2" pieces of construction paper, 7 per person.
> Duplicate pattern on resource sheet.
> Prepare a poster listing the corporal works of mercy:
> > *Feed the hungry.*
> > *Give drink to the thirsty.*
> > *Clothe the naked.*
> > *Shelter the homeless.*
> > *Visit the sick.*
> > *Visit the imprisoned.*
> > *Bury the dead.*
> Prepare a poster listing the spiritual works of mercy:
> > *Help the sinner.*
> > *Teach the ignorant*
> > *Counsel the doubtful.*
> > *Comfort the sorrowful.*
> > *Bear wrongs patiently.*
> > *Forgive injuries.*
> > *Pray for the living and the dead.*

Guide

Fourteen is a number associated with a special day in February. Ask the participants to name the holiday. Valentine's Day is the answer! This February 14 holiday focuses on a specific theme. Invite the group to name the topic highlighted on Valentine's Day. This time the answer is love.

Tell the learners that there are fourteen guides for living, also connected to the theme of love, that Christians have observed for hundreds of years. Invite someone to name the fourteen precepts known as the "works of mercy."

There are two parts to the works of mercy: Seven corporal works of mercy and seven spiritual works of mercy. Explain that the word corporal means "of the body" while the word spiritual refers to "things of the spirit, or of the soul."

Display the two lists and review the fourteen works of mercy. Ask the group to name ways that the two lists are alike and ways that they are different. Both sets of seven works are based on showing love for God, self, and others. Sometimes the spiritual works are of a personal nature, while the corporal works involve public acts. Note that all fourteen works of mercy are intended to bring about God's Kingdom. Compare and contrast the two lists until the learners run out of ideas.

Extend the activity by discussing specific examples of ways to carry out—or live—the works of mercy. Remind the learners that these fourteen directives must be woven into our lives and carried out every day—not just when we are reminded of them. Though Valentine's Day is a special time to show love, every day is an opportunity to remember that we are loved by God and to show God's love to others. The fourteen works of mercy challenge us to put love into action. We should try to serve God, to worship, to praise, and to pray, seven days a week.

Invite the group to make prayer prompters as a way to help them remember to observe the works of mercy. Show an example of a completed prayer prompter and demonstrate the process for constructing this teaching tool. Select one long piece of construction paper. Fold the long paper into thirds, with four inches in each section. Using the pattern provided, cut two vertical slits in the center section of the strip. The slits should be two and one-half inches long and three inches apart. Fold the paper on the dotted lines indicated on the pattern. The prayer prompter should now be triangular in shape. Glue the tab in place at the bottom of the paper.

Choose seven pieces of four-inch by two-inch paper. Using a pen, write one day of the week, Sunday through Saturday, in the left-hand corner of each piece. Next, write one of the corporal works of mercy on the right side of the strip. It will be helpful to write the word "corporal" or to print the letters "CW" somewhere on this side of the strip. Turn the construction paper pieces over and repeat the process, only this time write the days of the week on the left side and print one of the spiritual works of mercy on the right side of each paper. Also include the word "spiritual" or print the letters "SW" on each strip.

Insert the seven slips in order, with Sunday at the top, into the center section of the prompter.

Distribute the supplies and guide the group as they construct their own prayer prompters. Once the projects are completed, provide instructions for using the teaching tool.

On Sunday, pray the first prayer related to the corporal works of mercy. Ask for God's guidance in sharing love in this specific situation. Remove the slip, turn it over, and place it on the bottom of the prayer prompter. It may be necessary to slide the remaining six strips to the top. Pray the second idea on Monday, now at the top, and continue in this manner every day of the week. At the end of seven days, the first strip, Sunday, will be on top of the prompter with the seven spiritual works of mercy displayed. At this point, repeat the process.

Prayer Prompter

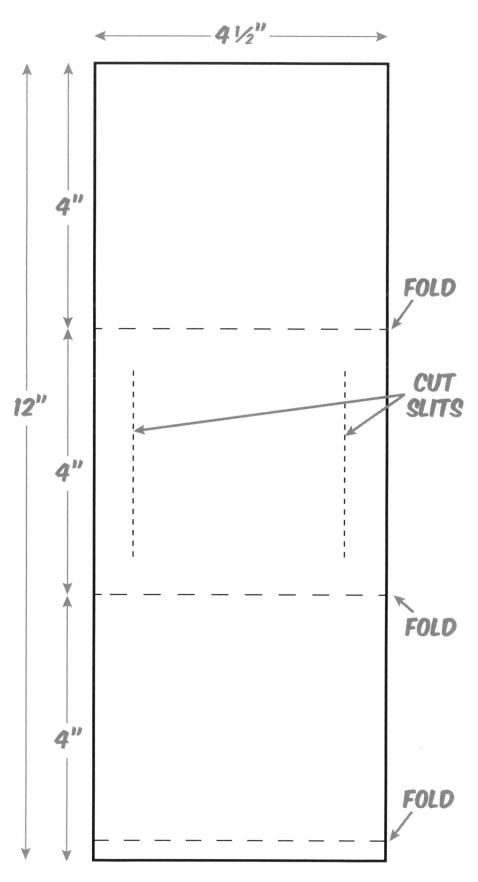

4 ½"

12"

4"

4"

4"

FOLD

CUT SLITS

FOLD

FOLD

⑮ Stations of the Cross

Goal

By illustrating the Stations of the Cross with cartoons, participants will understand the relevance of this traditional prayer in today's world.

Gather

> Cartons, 15 (optional)
> Glue
> Magazines and newspapers, recycled
> Markers
> Newsprint
> Paper, white, 15 pieces (optional)
> Resource sheet:
>> Stations of the Cross
> Scissors
> Tape, masking

Guide

The Stations of the Cross is a prayer that has been an enduring source of inspiration through the years. Of late, however, this beautiful and meaningful devotional has been practiced less and less by young people who find it difficult to make an appropriate application of Jesus' sufferings to the world today and to their own daily lives. This learning activity is intended to bridge the gap between youthful experience and mature meditation on the Stations of the Cross. A fifteenth station, Resurrection, has been added by many Christians, since the prayer is meaningless unless the Living Christ is kept in mind.

Ask the group to name the fifteen parts to the Stations of the Cross. Help the learners by encouraging them to think about the things that could have happened as Jesus walked to Calvary. Don't be concerned with right or wrong answers or any particular order at this time. Allow the students to talk through the possible events. For example, Jesus met people on the way and stopped to talk with them; Jesus got tired and thirsty; Jesus was given a cross to carry; Jesus may have been sad, and so on. Write the group's ideas on newsprint. Allow time for all ideas.

Once the participants have exhausted the possibilities for identifying the Stations, share the following list with the group. Read the Stations together.

▷

Stations of the Cross

1. *Jesus is condemned to death*

2. *Jesus takes up his cross*

3. *Jesus falls the first time*

4. *Jesus meets his mother, Mary*

5. *Simon helps Jesus carry his cross*

6. *Veronica wipes the face of Jesus*

7. *Jesus falls the second time*

8. *Jesus speaks to the women*

9. *Jesus falls a third time*

10. *Jesus is stripped of his clothes*

11. *Jesus is nailed to the cross*

12. *Jesus dies*

13. *Jesus is taken down from the cross*

14. *Jesus is buried*

15. *Jesus rises from the dead.*

Check to see how many stations the students identified in their brainstorming. Verbally reward their efforts!

Invite the students to think about ways in which the fifteen Stations of the Cross relate to events in today's world. Brainstorm how each Station parallels a contemporary situation. For example:

› "Jesus is condemned to death" might remind the group of starving children across the world.
› "Jesus Falls" may suggest a memory of an elderly person alone and frightened.
› "Jesus Dies" could prompt stories of gang violence.

Tell the group that they will have the opportunity to use these ideas to create cartoons depicting the Stations of the Cross as they relate to everyday life.

The meditations found on the resource sheet could be used before creating the cartoons to give the learners ideas for their projects.

Organize the learners into fifteen groups and assign one station to each team. As the background for the cartoon strips, distribute a sheet of newsprint, a piece of white construction paper, or a cardboard carton to each small group. Provide markers and direct the students to print the words of their assigned Station on the background material. Suggest that each group draw several, possibly four, frames for the cartoon strip. If boxes are used, one frame could be created on each side of a carton. Provide magazines, newspapers, scissors, and glue. Tell the participants to use these materials to illustrate the scenes they wish to depict. Pictures and words may be cut from magazines and newspapers and attached to the frames and words and images can be drawn on the cartoon strips as well. Guide the group as they work on their projects.

Once the activity is completed and clean-up has taken place, display the cartoon strips, in order, around the room. Tape newsprint or construction paper sheets to the walls, or stack or line up the cartons. Ask the group to share their strips and to talk about what they learned by participating in a project related to this traditional prayer.

Stations of the Cross

1. Jesus Is Condemned to Death

There are many people on death row, Lord. Many of our people are homeless, they live in the street. We look down on them. Condemned, Lord! Who gave us that right? To stand above another creature, and look down, to judge. How powerful we feel. How unlike you we are.

2. Jesus Takes His Cross

The cross looks more powerful than you, Lord. The elderly are forgotten, Lord. People are dying everywhere from gun violence. Too many crosses. Yet you are more powerful. Love makes it lighter.

3. Jesus Falls

The youth of our world give in to drugs and sexual pressures. People are put down and called names. It hurts to fall and be broken, Lord. Drained of all your dignity... I thought he always wanted me to stand straight! Help me fit my idea of "straight" to yours, Lord.

4. Jesus Meets His Mother

There are good people, God, giving and helping those who are hurting. Words can be a comfort for those in pain. Mother and son have given completely. Love makes you feel a real part of another. You feel their pain and their joys, and they feel yours.

5. Simon Helps Jesus Carry the Cross

Soup kitchens, shelters for the homeless, clothing centers, hospice care, a good friend. These are all cross-carrying helpers, Lord. People reaching out, people caring enough to give. When there are two to carry the cross it seems lighter. We don't each have a separate cross, Lord. Teach us to help one another.

6. Veronica Wipes the Face of Jesus

Lord, thank you for our families and friends, they help to wipe the tears. They stop and look into our eyes and take the time to care and love. It takes courage—to look into the face of another —to help. The other is Jesus.

7. Jesus Falls Again

Broken again!

8. Jesus Meets the Women

Thank you, God, for the feminine influence. For mothers and grandmothers, for sisters and daughters. You say reflect about yourselves, your children, your lives. I am doing God's will.

9. Jesus Falls a Third Time

Three times, Lord! No person could stand this... straight, Lord! Killing and cheating, lying and hating. Do you mean supernaturally straight, with your grace? Is that how we are to stand? Not as others see, but as you see.

10. Jesus Is Stripped of His Clothes

They have nothing, Lord. They are poor and destitute. Freedom is gone. Everything I think belongs to me has been ripped off. Sometimes, being stripped is to be free, free from things, free to love deeply.

11. Jesus Is Crucified

Only pure love can be rooted this deep, deeper than nails could place it. No greater love, to die for a friend.

12. Jesus Dies

All human life must come to an end; we must all face death. May we look at the end of life as a gift, a passage that brings us to you, our God.

13. Jesus Is Taken Down

To help another person out, wipe a tear, give a smile... these are the ways we learn to love as you did. When we become like you we allow ourselves to be moved by another.

14. Jesus Is Buried

The tomb wasn't even Jesus' own. Help us understand your life, so that we, too, can rise.

15. Jesus Rises from the Dead

A newborn baby... flowers in spring time... two people deeply in love with each other... a mother or father with their child... the break of dawn. You are alive! You have come back and are with us always! Make all creation as one.

16 Old Testament Prophets

Goal

By surveying the prayers of the Old Testament prophets and using selected verses to construct a Ribbon Banner, participants will gain a better understanding of God.

Gather

- Bibles
- Dowel rod, 20 inches
- Glue
- Markers, fine-point black permanent
- Newsprint
- Paper
- Pencils
- Ribbon, 1-inch wide x 1 yard long - 16 pieces, assorted colors
- Scissors
- Tape, masking

Guide

A prophet is a person who responds to God's call, even in the face of great difficulties. Prophets keep the covenant and do God's loving will. All people are invited by God to be prophets in the world.

A prophet does not tell the future but is called by God to speak out and to remind people how God wants them to live. A prophet encourages people to obey God's law and to act justly.

The prophetic books of the Old Testament reflect the human experiences of suffering, sadness, and discouragement. The messages of the prophets help us remember that the greatest spiritual growth of the Jewish people took place during their lowest and most discouraging times.

The prophets had much to say about how to live life in tenderness, justice, and close union with God. These instructions can be better understood by exploring the prayers of the prophets and by remembering the prophet's desire for God's people.

Use this activity to offer participants a vision of hope to help them cope with the disappointments and discouragements they may experience. Challenge the learners to live out the message of the prophets and to heed their words of prayer.

Organize the class into sixteen pairs or small groups. Distribute Bibles, paper, and pencils, and assign each group one of the sixteen prophetic books of the Old Testament:

1. Isaiah	7. Amos	13. Zephaniah
2. Jeremiah	8. Obadiah	14. Haggai
3. Ezekiel	9. Jonah	15. Zechariah
4. Daniel	10. Micah	16. Malachi
5. Hosea	11. Nahum	
6. Joel	12. Habakkuk	

➤

Invite the groups to skim through their assigned book. Encourage the learners to write down statements about prayer, actual prayers, and prophetic advice on how people should live their lives. Allow time for the groups to work on this part of the project. After the teams have collected several statements, re-gather the large group. Ask each cluster to read two or three passages from their prophetic book and invite the class to select one of the references to be used to create a ribbon banner. Write the chosen verse on a piece of newsprint. Continue this process until all groups have had a turn to report. The following passages may be used as examples, if additional ideas are needed.

Isaiah 12:1

On that day, in prayer you will say:
I give you thanks, O Lord;
though you have been angry with me,
your anger has abated, and you have consoled me.

Jeremiah 31:33

I will place my law within them, and write it
upon their hearts;
I will be their God, and they shall be my people.

Ezekiel 37:14

I will put my spirit in you that you may live,
and I will settle you upon your land;
thus, you shall know that I am the Lord.
I promised, and I will do it, says the Lord.

Daniel 2:23

To you O God of my fathers,
I pray in thanksgiving,
because you have given me
wisdom and strength.
For it is love that I desire,
not sacrifice,
and knowledge of God rather than holocausts.

Joel 2:27

Remember always, I am the Lord your God,
and there is no other; my people shall never more
be put to shame.

Amos 6:1

Woe to the complacent and overconfident.

Obadiah 1:15

As you have done,
so, shall it be done to you.

Jonah 2:3

For out of my prayer I called to you Lord,
and you answered me;
from my distress I cried for help,
and you heard my voice.

Micah 6:8

The Lord your God asks only this:
Only to do right, to love goodness,
and to walk humbly with your God.

Nahum 1:7

The Lord is good,
a refuge on the day of distress;
He takes care of those who have recourse to him.

Habakkuk 3:19

God, my Lord, is my strength;
he makes my feet swift as those of hinds
and enables me to go upon the heights.

Zephaniah 2:3

Seek the Lord, all you humble of the earth,
seek justice, seek humility.

Haggai 1:13

I am with you, says the Lord.

Zechariah 10:1

Pray of the Lord for your needs.
For he sends the pouring rain in the spring
season! Have we not all one Father?
Has not one God created us?
Why then do we break faith with each other,
violating the covenant?

Malachi 2:10

Have we not all one Father? Has not one God
created us? Why then do we break faith with each
other, violating the covenant?

Once sixteen passages have been collected and written down on the newsprint, distribute the ribbon and markers, one set per group. Invite each group to print the selected verse, or a summary of it, on one side of the ribbon. Tell the teams to print the prophet, chapter, and verse on the back of the ribbon.

➤

Collect the ribbons as they are completed, and glue the tops of them around a long dowel rod. Be sure the verses all face the same direction. Display the ribbon banner for all to see. Invite the participants to share what they learned from the prophetic messages and how these Old Testament words relate to their lives today.

Talk together about ways young people can speak out against injustice to be prophetic. Ask questions like: Why does being a prophet take courage? Do you believe that you have been chosen by God to do something that only you can do? How can you be a prophet of hope, like Ezekiel, during challenging times in your family?

In closing, pray the following verses from Jeremiah 14:5,9 with the group:

> *"I chose you before I gave you life, and before you were born I selected you to be a prophet to the nations;"*

> *"Listen, I place my words in your mouth."*

Front:	Pray to the Lord for your needs.
Back:	Zechariah 10:1

On that day, in prayer you will say: I give you thanks, O Lord; though you have been angry with me, your anger has abated, and you have consoled me.

I will place my law within them, and write it upon their hearts; I will be their God, and they shall be my people.

I will put my spirit in you that you may live, and I will settle you upon your land; thus, you shall know that I am the Lord.

To you O God of my fathers, I pray in thanksgiving, because you have given me wisdom and strength. For it is love that I desire, not sacrifice, and knowledge of God rather than holocausts.

Remember always, I am the Lord your God, and there is no other; my people shall never more be put to shame.

Woe to the complacent and overconfident.

As you have done, so, shall it be done to you.

For out of my prayer I called to you Lord, and you answered me; from my distress I cried for help, and you heard my voice.

The Lord your God seeks only this: Only to do right, to love goodness, and to walk humbly with your God.

The Lord is good, a refuge on the day of distress: He takes care of those who have recourse to him.

God, my Lord, is my strength; he makes my feet swift as those of hinds and enables me to go upon the heights.

Seek the Lord, all you humble of the earth, seek justice, seek humility.

I am with you, says the Lord.

Pray of the Lord for your needs. For he sends the pouring rain in the spring season! Have we not all one Father? Has not one God created us? Why then do we break faith with each other, violating the covenant?

Have we not all one Father? Has not one God created us? Why then do we break faith with each other, violating the covenant?

To you O God of my fathers, I pray in thanksgiving, because you have given me wisdom and strength. For it is love that I desire, not sacrifice, and knowledge of God rather than holocausts.

⑰ Saint Patrick's Prayers

Goal

After reviewing the prayers of Saint Patrick, whose feast day is celebrated March 17, participants will use writing and movement to offer their own prayers to God.

Gather

> Candle
> Equipment to play recording
> Matches
> Paper
> Pencils
> Recording of tranquil background music
> Resource sheet:
>> "Irish Blessing Prayer Gestures"

Guide

Prayer is important! And prayer was especially important to the saint whose feast day is celebrated on March 17. Ask the group to name this person: Saint Patrick. Share the story of Saint Patrick with the students, telling of his deep faith and his work to bring the Gospel to the people of Ireland. Read the group some of the writings of Patrick to help illustrate his life of prayer and his commitment to God. Invite the participants to express their commitment to God through creative writing and gestural interpretation activities.

Explain that very little is known about Saint Patrick's early life. As a boy of fourteen, Patrick was carried off by raiders and taken to Ireland as a slave. In his captivity Patrick turned to God. In his writings Saint Patrick tells us:

> *"The love of God and his mercy grew in me more and more, as did the faith, and my soul was roused, so that, in a single day, I have said as many as a hundred prayers and in the night nearly the same."*

Prayer was Patrick's life. He would often go to distant places to speak with God. One of the best known places where Patrick spent time in prayer and fasting was Croagh Patrick or "Saint Patrick's mountain." In fact, Patrick said:

> *"I prayed in the woods, in the fields, and on the mountain, even before dawn."*

Patrick gave until he had no more to give, and he was happy to see himself poor with Jesus. He knew that poverty and prayer would bring him closer to God. One of the reasons for Patrick's great holiness was his deep humility. He wrote a book called the "Confessions," in which he speaks about his relationship with God.

➤

"I give unceasing thanks to my God, who kept me faithful in the day of my testing. Today I can offer him sacrifice with confidence, giving myself as a living sacrifice to Christ, who kept me safe through all my trials."

"God showed me… I might be bold enough to take up so holy and wonderful a task, and imitate in some way those whom Jesus has so long ago foretold as heralds of his Gospel."

Before his death Patrick wrote:

"It happened in Ireland that those who never had a knowledge of God, but until now always worshiped idols, have now been made people of Christ, and are called children of God; that the sons and daughters of the kings of the Irish are seen as followers of Christ."

Prayer was an important part of Saint Patrick's life! Ask the students if prayer is important in their lives. How do they pray? When do they pray? Where do they prayer? How do they know that God hears their prayers? How do they listen to God speaking to them? Share reactions to these questions.

Distribute paper and pencils. Encourage the learners to respond to some of the writings of Patrick by inviting them to record their thoughts and feelings on statements such as:

› *How do you live the Gospel?*
› *What idols do you have in your own life?*
› *Who are the people walking with you and showing you the way?*
› *When has your soul been roused?*
› *How does a soul become roused?*
› *Has there ever been a time when your life was a never-ending prayer? What was the circumstance?*
› *Has there been a time of deep trial when God remained very near? How have you thanked God?*

After the students record their responses, allow time for sharing and discussion. Give the students an opportunity to speak freely of their own experiences in relation to the experiences of Saint Patrick.

Continue the activity by offering a time of silence for personal reflection. Give the participants an opportunity to share their own life experiences by writing prayers to God. Light the candle and play soft music in the background.

As a way to celebrate the life and work of Saint Patrick, conclude by reciting a traditional Irish blessing and interpreting it with gestures and sign language. Read the prayer to the group:

May the road rise to meet you.
May the wind be always at your back.
May the sun shine warm upon your face,
The rain fall soft upon your fields.
And, until we meet again,
May God hold you in the palm of his hand.

Using the suggestions on the resource sheet, interpret each word with movement and ask the group to repeat the action.

Irish Blessing Hand Gestures (1/2)

May: Extend hands in front of body, palms up.

Road: Move hands in front of body in zigzag motion.

Rise: Lift hands over head.

To: Direct the right index finger towards, and then touch, the left index fingertip which is pointing up.

Meet: Bring both hands together from the sides so the palms meet, fingers bent in and thumb and index finger pointing out.

You: Point one index finger out.

May: Extend hands in front of body.

Wind: Hold the hands high, palms together, the left slightly lower than the right; move them towards the left in several sweeping motions.

Be: Place the tip of the index finger at the mouth; move it forward, still upright.

Always: Make a clockwise circle in front of the body with the index finger, palm facing up.

At: Hold the left hand in front of the body, palm out. Strike the back of the left hand with the tips of the right hand, both hands pointing upward.

Your: Face the right palm out, directing it forward.

Back: Touch back with right hand crossing over left shoulder.

May: Extend hands in front of body.

Sun: Draw a clockwise circle in the air.

Shine: Open palms facing each other with tips pointing up. Wiggle fingers.

Warm: Place the right fist in front of the mouth, palm in, and open the hand gradually as it moves slightly up and out.

Upon: Point up with the right index finger.

Your: Face the palm out, directing it forward.

Face: Using the right index finger, trace a circle in front of the face.

Rain: Let both curved hands drop down several times in short, quick motions.

Fall: Form a "V" with two fingers of the right hand and place it in a standing position on the left palm; let the "V" fall, palm down, into the left hand.

Irish Blessing Hand Gestures (2/2)

Soft: Point open hands upward, then draw them down, fingers together.

Upon: Point up with the right index finger.

Your: Face the palm out, directing it forward.

Fields: Rub the fingertips of both hands with the thumb as if feeling soil; make a counter-clockwise circle with the right open hand, palm down.

And: Place the right hand in front of body, fingers spread apart, and point left. Draw the hand to the right, closing the tips.

Until: Direct the right index finger in a forward arc and touch the left index finger which is pointing up.

We: Place the index finger at the right shoulder and circle it forward and around until it touches the left shoulder.

Meet: Bring both hands together from the sides so the palms meet, fingers bent in and thumb and index finger point out.

Again: The right curved hand faces up, then turns and moves to the left so that the fingertips touch the left palm which is pointing forward with the palm facing right. Repeat action several times.

May: Extend hands in front of body.

God: Point the right index finger forward in front of you, draw it up and back down, opening the palm which is facing left.

Hold: Both open hands, palms up, move from right to left in front of body.

You: Point one index finger out.

In: Place the closed fingertips of the right hand into the left half-circled hand.

Palm: Point to left palm with right index finger.

His: Point the right index finger forward in front of you, draw it up and back down, opening the palm which is facing left.

Hand: Stroke the back of the left hand with the right hand and reverse the action.

⑱ The Pharisee and the Publican

Goal

To review the parable of the "Pharisee and the Publican," found in Luke 18:9-14, and to make and use puppets to learn the proper attitude for prayer.

Gather

> Bibles

> Craft sticks or dowel rods

> Fabric scraps

> Fake fur or yarn

> Felt

> Glue

> Paper tubes, various sizes

> Scissors

Guide

In the Gospel of Luke, Jesus not only teaches his disciples a pattern for prayer—the Lord's Prayer found in chapter 11:1-4—he also provides his followers with instructions for the proper attitude for prayer. In Luke 18:9-15, the passage commonly known as "The Parable of the Pharisee and the Publican (tax collector)," Jesus instructs us to pray honestly and humbly. Jesus reminds us to pray sincerely, like the tax collector, not self-righteously like the Pharisee.

Look up Luke 18: 9-14 in a Bible and read the verses to the students. Offer various translations of God's Word and invite the participants to compare the passage in different versions.

Tell the group that they will make puppets from paper tubes and that they will write a script or improvise actions to tell the story of the Pharisee and the Publican.

Turn paper tubes of any size into puppets. Use paper towel tubes or toilet paper rolls for average sized puppets or try wrapping paper or carpet rolls for giant characters. Demonstrate the process for constructing Pharisee and publican puppets.

Select a tube. Form the puppet face by cutting a piece of felt and gluing it to the top one-third of the cardboard. Make facial features from felt scraps and glue them in place. Attach yarn or fake fur to the top of the tube for hair.

Glue a piece of felt around the remainder of the tube to serve as the undergarment. Layers of fabric in contrasting or complementary colors can be added as overgarments.

Make arms from strips of cloth or felt and glue them to the sides of the tube.

Apply a craft stick to the inside back of the tube to serve as the rod by which the puppet is operated.

▷

If felt is not available, use construction paper instead. The facial features may be drawn on with marker. Substitute tissue paper for fabric to form the outer garments.

Provide the supplies and guide the group as each person creates his or her own set of characters.

Write a puppet show to act out the Luke 18:9-14 passage. The story needs to have a beginning, a middle, and an end. These can also be called Acts I, II, and III.

Start by deciding the action that takes place in each scene. Write short, simple dialogue between the characters. In Act I, the beginning, establish the time and place. Introduce the main characters and their relationship to each other. Establish the conflict. During Act II, the middle, list the series of events that move towards the climax, or confrontation, of the conflict. In the end, Act III, resolve the conflict in a believable way. Determine the props and scenery that will be needed to enhance the story. Act out the story, using the tube puppet characters.

Since the parable of the Pharisee and the Publican is familiar to people of all ages, use the tube puppets to improvise the Bible passage. To improvise means to compose and to perform without preparation. There is no specific script and no right or wrong way to tell the story. Read or review the account found in Luke 18:9-14 and instruct the puppeteers to portray the action, with or without words. Allow the participants to take turns playing various parts.

Conclude the session with the prayer of a publican rather than a prayer of a Pharisee—that is, an honest, humble request for God's help in sustaining a proper attitude of prayer.

⑲ Gospels

Goal

Since there are nineteen letters in the names of the four Gospels—Matthew, Mark, Luke, and John—participants will study these books to review nineteen passages related to Jesus' teachings on prayer.

Gather

> Bibles, one per person
> Paper
> Pencils

Guide

Ask the participants to name the four Gospels (Matthew, Mark, Luke and John). Challenge the group to guess what the number nineteen has to do with these books. Give the students an opportunity to respond. If no one offers the correct answer, state that there are nineteen letters in the words Matthew, Mark, Luke, and John. Count the letters together.

Invite the participants to recall some of their favorite stories from the Gospels. Distribute Bibles and encourage the learners to look up various texts. Once the students have had an opportunity to share their selections, continue by asking the group to talk about Jesus' teachings on prayer. What examples and instructions are recorded in these New Testament books? Allow time for discussion.

Distribute paper and pencils. Explain that the group will search the first four books of the New Testament to study nineteen passages related to the theme of prayer.

➤

The Gospel of John

Ask the students to look up five passages in their Bibles. Invite discussion and sharing on the message of each text.

- *John 2:13-22 - Jesus cleanses the Temple*
- *John 10:10 - "...I came that they may have life, and have it abundantly."*
- *John 13:1-15 - Jesus washes the disciples' feet*
- *John 14:6 - "I am the way, and the truth, and the life..."*
- *John 15:1-10 - Jesus the true vine*

Explain that one of the most important insights of John's Gospel is that John invites all people to live life to the fullest. Stress that God not only desires to give fullness of life but also helps us to achieve this abundant life. Invite the participants to sit quietly for a minute or two. Ask them to read the scripture texts again—silently and meditatively. Pause for a moment or two of reflection.

The Gospel of Mark

Invite the students to close their eyes for a moment. Ask them to "just be" in God's presence. Tell the group that they will use Mark's Gospel to help them pray over the stories of Jesus' last days on earth.

Have the participants look up the following passages in their Bibles. Ask them to write down the main message of each text. Allow time for work and sharing.

- *Mark 14:22-26 - "This is my body..."*
- *Mark 14:32-41 - The Garden of Gethsemane*
- *Mark 15:16-20 - Jesus crowned with thorns*
- *Mark 15-21-37 - Jesus crucified*
- *Mark 16:1-19 - The empty tomb*

The Gospel of Luke

Encourage the students to find and to read five Scripture passages in the Gospel of Luke. Ask them to make note of how these texts speak of prayer and of the strength believers gain by having God in their lives.

- *Luke 4:1-13 - The temptation of Jesus*
- *Luke 9:18-22 - Peter's confession*
- *Luke 19:1-10 - Zacchaeus' conversion*
- *Luke 22:36-39 - Jesus' agony in the garden*
- *Luke 24:13-35 - The Emmaus walk*

The Gospel of Matthew

Invite the students to use the Gospel of Matthew to pray over important aspects of Jesus' life. Encourage students to share findings and to cite the importance of each passage for their own personal lives. Ask the students to write down the main point of each passage.

- *Matthew 4:18-22 - The calling of the disciples*
- *Matthew 9:1-8 - Healing of the paralyzed man*
- *Matthew 15:32-38 - Multiplication of the loaves and the fish*
- *Matthew 17:1-9 - Jesus transfigured*

Once the Scripture study is completed, encourage the students to read a passage from one of the Gospels every night as a way of getting closer to Jesus through prayer.

⓴ Fingers and Toes

Goal

By participating in a handprint/footprint banner painting project, participants will identify people who need their prayers.

Gather

- Bedsheet or cotton fabric, white
- Chalkboard and chalk or newsprint and markers
- Dishpan
- Markers, permanent
- Paint, tempera in variety of colors
- Soap, liquid
- Tape, duct or masking
- Towels, paper
- Water

Guide

Prayer is an important part of daily life. Without God things can seem impossible. Prayer is part of a friendship that exists between God and God's people.

Lifting up mind and heart to God is one definition of prayer. Yet, prayer, like poetry, is hard to define. Write twenty definitions of prayer, using the examples provided plus other ideas, on a piece of newsprint:

- *A hymn, a love song*
- *Being in the company of one who deeply loves you*
- *Telling God you're sorry*
- *Being dissolved into someone greater than yourself*
- *A response for God's love*
- *Thanking God for God's gifts*
- *Asking God for something*
- *Communication with God*

Ask the participants to read the statements and to choose the one that seems closest to their own interpretation of prayer. Invite the students to share with the group why they chose a particular answer.

Some of the definitions describe reasons for praying. Remind the group of the simple formula containing the four parts of prayer—ACTS—adoration, contrition or confession, thanksgiving, and supplication. Tell them that they will participate in a banner making activity focusing on prayers of supplication.

➤

Ask someone to define the word supplication. Explain that supplication means asking for or requesting something from God. When we pray, we communicate with a loving and caring God who wants nothing more than to give us what is best for our lives. Even when specific prayers don't seem to be granted, assure the group that God hears and answers every prayer. Invite the students to share prayer requests that they have made and answers that they have received. Examples could be getting an A on a test, making the team, and having a part in the school play.

Now ask if anyone has prayed a prayer of supplication on behalf of someone else. Of course, the answer will be yes. Examples might include praying that mom would get better, asking God to be with a grandparent on a trip, and requesting help for dad during a big project. Next, brainstorm a list of different groups of people who need to be remembered in prayer. Try to guide the suggestions to categories of people, rather than specific names. Challenge the students to come up with a least twenty different groups of people who need God's help. Write the student's responses on a sheet of newsprint.

The following list could serve as a guide for the activity:

1. The hungry

2. The homeless

3. The unemployed

4. Parent(s)

5. Teenagers

6. Abused children

7. People in war

8. People with HIV and AIDS

9. People who are dying alone

10. People who make racist remarks

11. Drug addicts

12. Young people who are in gangs

13. Young adults who try to commit suicide

14. Teachers

15. Health care workers

16. Social workers

17. People who work for the rights and freedom of all people

18. Missionaries

19. People who teach and live the Gospel

20. All of us.

Once a list has been compiled, invite the students to take part in a banner making project as a way to remember people who need their prayers. Ask the group to guess why the number twenty has been used throughout this activity. Then ask the participants to name the way they learned to count, or the way they counted when they were very young—probably on their fingers and toes! Tell the group that they will make a unique banner by painting their fingers and toes on a large piece of fabric. Each finger and toe will represent a person who needs to be remembered in prayer.

Spread the bedsheet on the floor in the center of a large room. Note that this project can be done outdoors, weather permitting, for less indoor clean up! Tape the corners and the sides of the cloth to the floor. Pour each color of tempera paint into a separate dishpan. Place only enough paint in the pans to cover palms of hands and bottoms of feet. Add a small amount of liquid soap to the paint to aid clean-up. Place the filled dishpans around the sides of the sheet.

Invite the banner makers to remove their shoes and socks. Instruct one or two participants at a time to choose a color and to carefully step into the dishpan containing it. Direct each person to slowly walk across the sheet. Be sure that the toes on each foot are imprinted on the fabric. Provide wet paper towels at the end of the walk and assist with clean-up. Continue this procedure until everyone has had a turn.

➤

Next, add handprints to the banner by instructing one or two pupils at a time to choose a color of paint and to carefully place both hands into the dishpan containing it. Direct each person to press his or her hands onto the fabric, making sure that each finger forms a clear print. Provide clean-up assistance. As the banner is being created remind the students that there are as many people who need prayers of supplication as there are fingers and toes on the banner. Note that when one color touches another, a change takes place. Comment that when we pray for Jesus to touch people's lives, changes can take place too.

Once all of the participants have had an opportunity to add hand and foot prints to the banner, set the piece aside to dry. Refer to the brainstormed list and ask the class to pick twenty "people" to include on the banner—one representing each finger and each toe! When the banner is completely dry, invite the students to write the twenty words around or in twenty different hand or foot prints. Provide permanent markers for this purpose. Hang the completed project in a prominent location for all to see.

In closing, read the following passage, 1 John 4:7-16, from the writings of Saint John slowly and thoughtfully.

> Beloved,
> let us love one another, because love is from God;
> everyone who loves is born of God
> and knows God.
>
> Whoever does not love does not know God,
> for God is love.
>
> God's love was revealed among us in this way:
> God sent his only Son into the world
> so that we might live through him.
>
> In this is love,
> not that we loved God but that he loved us
> and sent his Son to be the atoning sacrifice
> for our sins.
>
> Beloved,
> since God loved us so much,
> we also ought to love one another.
>
> No one has ever seen God;
> if we love one another, God lives in us,
> and his love is perfected in us.
>
> By this we know that we abide in him
> and he in us, because he has given us of his Spirit.
>
> And we have seen and do testify
> that the Father has sent his Son
> as the Savior of the world.
>
> God abides in those who confess that
> Jesus is the Son of God, and they abide in God.
>
> So we have known and believe the love
> that God has for us.
>
> God is love,
> and those who abide in love abide in God,
> and God abides in them.

Conclude by offering a prayer for the twenty groups of people named on the hand and foot print banner. Invite the students to count them on fingers and toes while the prayer is being recited.

Resources

Caprio, Betsy. *Experiments In Prayer.* Notre Dame, IN: Ave Maria Press, 1973.

Cronin, Gaynell Bordes. *Holy Days and Holidays: Prayer Celebrations with Children* (2 volumes). San Francisco: Harper & Row, 1985, 1988.

Jessie, Karen. *Praying with Children Grades 4-6.* Villa Maria, PA: The Center for Learning, 1986.

Jones, Timothy and Jill Zook-Jones. *Prayer - Discovering What Scripture Says.* Wheaton, IL: Harold Shaw Publishers, 1993.

Manternach, Janaan with Carl J. Pfeifer. *And the Children Pray.* Notre Dame, IN: Ave Maria Press, 1989.

Mathson, Patricia. *Pray & Play: 28 Prayer Services and Activities for Children In K through Sixth Grade.* Notre Dame, IN: Ave Maria Press, 1989.

Rezy, Carol. *Liturgies for Little Ones: 38 Celebrations for Grades One to Three.* Notre Dame, IN: Ave Maria Press, 1978.

Smith, Judy Gattis. *Teaching Children about Prayer.* Prescott, AZ: Educational Ministries, 1988.

About the Author

Phyllis Vos Wezeman

As a religious educator, Phyllis Wezeman has served as Director of Christian Nurture at a downtown congregation in South Bend, Indiana, Executive Director of the Parish Resource Center of Michiana, and Program Coordinator for ecumenical as well as interfaith organizations in Indiana and Michigan.

In academics, Phyllis has been Adjunct Faculty in the Education Department at Indiana University South Bend and in the Department of Theology at the University of Notre Dame. She is an "Honorary Professor" of the Saint Petersburg (Russia) State University of Pedagogical Art where she has taught methods courses for extended periods on several occasions. She has also been guest lecturer at the Shanghai Teachers College in China.

As founder of the not-for-profit Malawi Matters, Inc., she develops and directs HIV & AIDS Education programs with thousands of volunteers in nearly 200 villages in Malawi, Africa including "Creative Methods of HIV & AIDS Education," "Culture & HIV-AIDS," and "Equipping Women/Empowering Girls."

Author or co-author of over 1,950 articles and books, she has written for over 80 publishers.

Phyllis served as President of Active Learning Associates, Inc.; a consultant or board member to numerous local and national organizations such as the American Bible Society, Church World Service, LOGOS, and the Peace Child Foundation; leader of a six-week youth exchange program to Russia and the Ukraine; and Project Director for four Lilley Worship Renewal grants. She is the recipient of three "Distinguished Alumni Awards" and recipient of the Aggiornamento Award from the Catholic Library Association.

Wezeman holds undergraduate degrees in Business, Communications, and General Studies from various institutions and an MS in Education from Indiana University South Bend.

Phyllis and her husband Ken (who met when they were in second and third grade in elementary school) have three children and their spouses, Stephanie (Jeff), David, and Paul (Deha), five grandchildren, Quin, Ayle, Lief, Ashley, and Jacob, and two great-grandsons, Maddox and Troy.

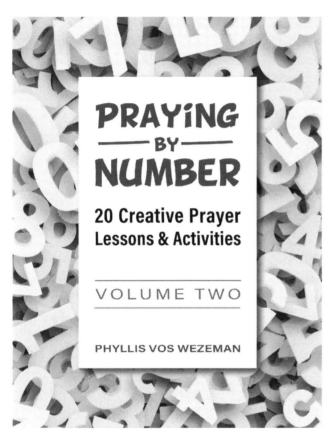

76 PAGES PER VOLUME • 8½"x11" • PW111

Praying by Number
Volume 2

*20 **More** Creative Prayer Lessons & Activities*

㉑ Meal Time Prayers
㉒ Evening Prayer
㉓ Psalm 23
㉔ 24 Hours
㉕ Feast Days
㉖ Letters of the Alphabet
㉗ Books of the New Testament
㉘ Promises of God
㉙ Syllables
㉚ Pieces of Silver
㉛ Prayer Guide
㉜ Names of Jesus
㉝ Jesus' Passion
㉞ Body Postures
㉟ Creation
㊱ Growth Chart
㊲ Symbols
㊳ Spontaneous Prayer
㊴ Prayer Chain
㊵ Wilderness Experiences

100 Creative Techniques for Teaching Bible Stories

In this treasure chest of fun ideas and activities, you'll find a wealth of practical possibilities for reviewing Scripture stories with the young and old. These easy-to-use techniques require very simple materials; for some you need only a Bible and your imagination. Each technique can be used for multiple purposes: to teach a prayer, to tell the story of a saint, or to enjoy a Scripture story in a new way. It is an ideal resource for catechists and religion teachers as well as for those preparing liturgies, summer programs, and intergenerational activities.

108 PAGES * 8½"x11" * PW101

Experience the Saints

Activities for Multiple Intelligences

Eight activities per saint, each based on a different learning intelligence. Includes whole family and general classroom guides, with reproducible handouts.

- Vol. 1: Patrick, James, Hildegard of Bingen * PW201
- Vol. 2: Francis, Clare, Margaret of Scotland * PW202
- Vol. 3: Joan of Arc, Thomas Becket, Agnes * PW203
- Vol. 4: Peter, Catherine of Siena, Scholastica * PW204

200 PAGES PER VOLUME * 8½"x11"

52 Interactive Bible Stories

A Collection of Action, Echo, Rhythm, and Syllable Stories

Participants will love these playful ways of expressing Scripture through a variety of storytelling techniques:. This delightful collection tells Bible stories in creative, interactive ways that will engage anyone from the toddlers through adulthood. They are a great way to add life to classes or retreat-like experiences. These playful stories involve the learner in the process and ensure that the Bible story is understood an internalized.

74 PAGES * 8½"x11" * PW100

Seasons by Step: A Week-by-Week Thematic Approach

Use these creative approaches to explore a theme in-depth over the course of a season through Scripture. Each includes **talking points for children's messages**, **at-home family activities**, **artwork** for weekly symbols, and more.

Know Chocolate for Lent *(Lent & Holy Week)*

Uses the growing and manufacturing process of chocolate as a metaphor for the growth of faith and discipleship in the Christian life. Adult formation materials for a parish-wide approach are sold separately. ● 80 PAGES ● LR119

God's Family Tree *(Lent & Holy Week)*
Tracing the Story of Salvation

Tells the story of God's people as they struggle to find faith and hope for life through the symbols of trees found in Scripture. Includes optional Easter pageant and classroom activities. ● 114 PAGES ● LR116

In the Name of the Master *(Advent/Christmas/Epiphany)*
Sharing the Story of Christ

Uses a variation of the Advent wreath that uses fruits as symbols for the many names of God's Masterpiece, Jesus. Help your kids & families go deeper as they light their Advent candles each week. ● 37 PAGES ● LR108

· ·

Joy to the World
International Christmas Crafts & Customs

Dozens of activities, from 12 countries that you can use again and again. Develop an appreciation for the contributions of the peoples of all lands and races to the celebration of Christmas. ● 159 PAGES ● 8½"x11" ● LR104

Ideas A-Z
Crafts & Activities for Advent, Christmas, & Epiphany

Offers different theme or learning approach for each letter of the alphabet. Great ideas for intergenerational activities, lesson plans, or worship experiences. ● 94 PAGES ● 8½"x11" ● PW102

Finding Your Way after Your Child Dies

Offers parents a comforting way to grieve. Easily adapted for use in small and large group settings such as a support group, prayer service, or family ministry session. ● 192 PAGES ● IC937005

http://pastoral.center/phyllis-vos-wezeman

 **The Pastoral Center** *Pastoral ministers serving pastoral ministers*

http://pastoral.center • resources@pastoralcenter.com • Call us at 844-727-8672 (M-F 9am-5pm CT)

Made in the USA
San Bernardino, CA
18 November 2018